NEP STUDENTS GUIDE FOR ENGLISH LITERATURE

A PRACTICAL RESOURCE FOR STUDENTS AND TEACHERS

DR. VISHWANATH BITE

Dedicated to

My Father, Shri. K. S. Bite

Who taught me

to be the best in whatever I want to be

&

my inspiring teachers and students

who have been instrumental in helping me grow and improve

every day in every way.

Contents

Introduction

Have you ever found yourself lost in the pages of a book, immersed in a world that feels more real than reality itself? Literature does that—it connects us to humanity in ways nothing else can. It's not just a collection of words on a page; it's an experience that shapes our thoughts, emotions, and understanding of the world around us. Whether you're an undergraduate student majoring in literature, an adult learner returning to education, or an educator looking for structured resources, this book is your guide to exploring the multifaceted universe of literature.

Literature is an intricate tapestry woven from countless human experiences, thoughts, and emotional threads. It encompasses everything from epic poetry's profound depth to satirical essays' sharp wit. Literature is a mirror reflecting the complexities of human existence, capturing moments of joy, sorrow, triumph, and despair in ways that resonate deeply with readers across time and space. By offering a broad spectrum of genres and forms, literature enables us to see the world through different lenses, fostering empathy and understanding.

The journey of literature is as old as civilisation itself. In ancient times, stories were passed down orally, becoming the bedrock of cultural identity and collective memory. These oral traditions eventually led to written texts, with early examples including the epic tales of Gilgamesh and Homer's "Iliad" and "Odyssey." As societies evolved, so did their literary expressions. The Middle Ages brought about chivalric romances and religious texts, while the Renaissance heralded a rebirth of classical ideas and the flourishing of drama and poetry. The print revolution further democratised literature, making it accessible to the masses and sparking new genres like the novel. Today, we find ourselves in the digital age, where literature continues to adapt, now embracing formats such as e-books and web serials, yet always remaining a vital part of cultural discourse.

But what makes literature genuinely magical is the role of the reader. Each reader brings their own experiences and emotions to a text, creating a unique interpretation that breathes new life into the written word. This collaborative interaction between author and audience transforms reading into a profoundly personal and dynamic experience. No two readers will interpret a story the same way, and that diversity of thought enriches our collective understanding of literature. Through this engagement, readers consume content and contribute to its ongoing evolution, ensuring that literature remains a living, breathing entity.

This book is designed to be your companion on a journey through the enchanting realm of literature. We will begin by exploring the primary genres, providing a framework to understand the fundamental categories such as fiction, poetry, and drama. Each genre will be dissected to reveal its unique characteristics and how it contributes to the broader literature landscape. You will learn how to identify and appreciate the nuances of each form, gaining insights that will enhance your reading experience.

Following our exploration of genres, we will delve into pivotal historical periods shaping literary development. From the classical antiquity of ancient Greece and Rome to the transformative eras of the Enlightenment and Romanticism and onward to the diverse voices of contemporary literature, we will trace the evolution of themes, styles, and narrative techniques. By contextualising literature within its historical framework, you will gain a deeper appreciation for the forces that have influenced writers and the works they created.

Critical analysis is another cornerstone of our journey. Understanding literature goes beyond mere reading; it requires us to engage critically with the text. We will introduce you to critical literary theories and methodologies, empowering you to dissect and interpret works with greater depth and sophistication. Concepts such as structuralism, post-structuralism, feminism, and post-colonialism will be explored, providing the analytical tools to tackle complex texts. These critical frameworks will help you uncover hidden meanings, question established interpretations, and develop your perspectives.

For those who seek to teach literature, this book offers valuable resources to support your curriculum development and pedagogical approach. Strategies for engaging students, fostering discussion, and encouraging creative thinking will be discussed. You will find practical tips for designing lessons that make literature accessible and exciting, transforming the classroom into a vibrant space for intellectual exploration.

In the final chapters, we will focus on the art of writing about literature. Effective communication of ideas is essential, whether crafting a research paper, presenting a literary review, or simply sharing your thoughts with fellow enthusiasts. We will guide you through constructing coherent arguments, using evidence to support your claims, and articulating your insights clearly and persuasively.

Ultimately, this book aims to equip you with the skills and knowledge to confidently navigate the rich and varied literature landscape. Whether you analyse a Shakespearean play, interpret a modernist poem, or explore the latest bestselling novel, you will find the tools you need within these pages. Our goal is to foster a more profound love and appreciation for literature, encouraging you to become not just a reader but a passionate advocate for the transformative power of the written word.

As you embark on this literary adventure, remember that studying literature is not just an academic exercise—it is a journey into the heart of being human. Through the stories we read and the analyses we conduct, we connect with the past, engage with the present, and envision the future. So, open your mind and heart, and let the world of literature enrich your life in ways you never imagined possible.

CHAPTER ONE

INTRODUCTION TO LITERATURE

"Understanding literature is fundamental for anyone who seeks to delve deeper into the human experience. Literature encompasses various written works, such as narratives, poems, and dramas, which go beyond mere record-keeping to evoke emotions, provoke thoughts, and convey profound messages. It draws from diverse cultures and historical periods, providing a rich tapestry of human expression that reflects society's values, struggles, and triumphs. The richness of literature lies in its ability to capture the essence of life through storytelling, making it an essential area of study for students, educators, and lifelong learners alike."

This chapter aims to provide a foundational understanding of literature by exploring its definition, scope, and historical significance. Readers will gain insights into the different genres and forms of literature, such as fiction, non-fiction, poetry, and drama, each with unique characteristics and purposes.

Additionally, the chapter will highlight the crucial role of readers in interpreting texts, emphasising the interactive nature of reading. By examining these elements, the chapter sets the stage for a comprehensive appreciation of literature, its societal functions, and its evolving nature through history.

Definition and Scope of Literature

Understanding what constitutes literature is a crucial starting point for anyone delving into this field. Literature can be broadly defined as written works that represent the human experience through narrative, poetic, and dramatic forms. It is an art form that transcends mere factual record-keeping, aiming to evoke emotions, provoke thoughts, and convey messages deeply rooted in the human psyche. The scope of literature encompasses a wide array of expressions from various cultures and historical periods, each contributing uniquely to our collective understanding of life, society, and the world around us.

At its essence, literature is classified into several genres and forms, each with distinct characteristics and purposes. By acknowledging these categories, students can gain a deeper appreciation for the diversity of literary works and their unique narratives and techniques, thereby enriching their understanding of literature.

One of the primary genres of literature is **fiction**, which involves imaginative storytelling. Fictional works are primarily created from the author's imagination rather than based strictly on facts. Within fiction, there are multiple sub-genres. For instance, **literary fiction** focuses on deep character development and thematic depth. It often challenges readers to think critically about societal norms, personal identity, and philosophical questions. Works by authors like Virginia Woolf and James Joyce fall into this category (*What Are Literary Genres? (plus 16 Types to Try)*, n.d.).

Another important genre is **historical fiction**, which blends imaginative narratives with historical events and figures. This genre provides insight into specific periods, making history accessible and engaging through compelling storylines. Authors such as Hilary Mantel and Ken Follett masterfully illustrate historical details while weaving intricate plots enthralling readers.

Science fiction explores futuristic concepts, alternate realities, and advanced science and technology. This genre allows authors and readers to speculate about potential futures and examine the ethical implications of technological advancements. Classic examples include works by Isaac Asimov and Philip K. Dick (*What Are Literary Genres? (plus 16 Types to Try)*, n.d.).

In contrast to science fiction's futuristic outlook, the **fantasy** genre delves into worlds of magic, mythical creatures, and epic adventures. J.R.R. Tolkien's "The Lord of the Rings" and J.K. Rowling's "Harry Potter" series epitomise this genre, creating richly detailed universes that captivate imaginations across generations.

Mystery and **thriller** genres revolve around suspenseful and often crime-related plots. These stories engage readers by presenting puzzles and challenges that protagonists must solve. Sir Arthur Conan Doyle's Sherlock Holmes series is an iconic example of mystery literature, while modern thrillers by authors like Gillian Flynn continue to evolve the genre (*SuperSummary*, n.d.).

Literature also includes **non-fiction** genres, where authors explore actual events, people, and facts. Nonfiction spans many subjects, including biographies, memoirs, essays, and academic texts. These works aim to inform, educate, and provide insights into real-world issues and experiences. For instance, Michelle Obama's memoir "Becoming" offers a personal perspective on her life and tenure as the First Lady of the United States.

Besides genre distinctions, literary forms are crucial in shaping how stories are told and received. **Novels** and **short stories** are common narrative forms used across many genres. Novels provide extensive character and plot development space, allowing for complex, multi-layered storytelling. Short stories, however, are concise and focus on capturing moments or highlighting specific themes within a limited word count.

Poetry is another significant form of literature characterised by its rhythmic and often symbolic language. Poems vary widely in structure and style, from sonnets and haikus to free verse and narrative poetry. Renowned poets like Emily Dickinson and Langston Hughes have used this form to express profound emotions and social commentary through carefully crafted verses.

Drama encompasses plays written for performance on stage or screen. This form relies on dialogue and action to develop characters and advance the plot. From classical works by William Shakespeare to contemporary plays by Lorraine Hansberry, drama showcases human conflict and resolution in a live setting, engaging audiences in a shared experience.

Students can cultivate a more nuanced appreciation for the written word by understanding the various genres and forms of literature. Each genre and form offers unique tools and perspectives that enrich readers' experience and broaden their analytical skills. Recognising these distinctions is essential for anyone looking to delve deeply into literary studies or enjoy the vast landscape of human storytelling.

Functions of Literature in Society

Literature is a profound mirror to society, reflecting and shaping its cultural values, educational methodologies, and social progress. Its significance goes beyond entertainment, delving into the core of human experience and societal development.

One of the primary roles of literature is its ability to reflect and mould cultural attitudes, values, and beliefs. Through stories, poems, plays, and essays, literature enables people to articulate their worldviews and share their experiences with others. This exchange preserves cultures and traditions and fosters an appreciation for diversity. For example, in ancient Greek literature, epic poems like Homer's "Iliad" and "Odyssey" provide insights into the heroism, honour, and gods integral to Greek culture. Such works have not only recorded historical values but have also influenced modern storytelling and philosophical thought.

Moreover, literature can be a powerful tool for fostering empathy and understanding. By immersing readers in the lives and struggles of characters from different backgrounds, literature helps build bridges between individuals and communities. This capacity for empathy is crucial in an increasingly globalised world where understanding diverse perspectives can lead to more harmonious coexistence. Characters like Harper Lee's Scout Finch in "To Kill a Mockingbird" allow readers to confront issues of race and justice, challenging them to empathise with those who face discrimination and marginalisation.

In addition to promoting empathy, literature often challenges prevailing assumptions and stereotypes, encouraging critical thinking. Works such as George Orwell's "1984" or Aldous Huxley's "Brave New World" force readers to question the status quo, explore new social possibilities, and envision different futures. These narratives serve as social and political commentary platforms, inspiring readers to reflect on their societies and consider paths toward improvement and equity.

Literature also plays a pivotal role in education, serving as a subject of study and a vehicle for broader learning. From early childhood through advanced studies, literature builds essential skills such as reading comprehension, critical analysis, and effective communication. Many students' first encounter with literature occurs in a classroom setting, where they are introduced to various genres, from classical novels to contemporary short stories. This academic exposure helps develop a love for reading and an ability to interpret complex texts and uncover more profound meanings.

Furthermore, literature is a conduit for historical knowledge, offering a window into past eras and civilisations. Historical texts and literary works from various periods allow us to understand how people lived, thought, and interacted with their world. Shakespeare's writings, for instance, provide valuable insights into the social norms and political dynamics of Elizabethan England. Similarly, Anne Frank's diaries offer a poignant perspective on life during the Holocaust, highlighting the human aspects of a tragic historical event.

By engaging with literature, readers can gain a nuanced understanding of societal issues, motivating them to advocate for social change. Literature can highlight injustices and advocate for the rights of underrepresented groups. Authors like James Baldwin and Maya Angelou illuminated racial and social inequalities in their writings, provoking readers to take action and pursue justice. Literature catalyses social movements through these narratives, inspiring individuals to strive for a more equitable and just society.

Another significant aspect of literature is its role in shaping and expressing individual and collective identities. It provides a platform for voices that might otherwise go unheard, enabling marginalised communities to share their stories and assert their place within the broader social fabric. For instance, postcolonial literature often explores themes of identity and resistance, giving voice to those who have been historically silenced. Chimamanda Ngozi Adichie's novels, like "Half of a Yellow Sun," convey the experiences of Nigerians during the Biafran War, contributing to a greater understanding of postcolonial African history and culture.

Literature continues to be relevant in contemporary society despite the rise of digital media and other forms of entertainment. It remains a vital part of educational curricula and public discourse, adapting to new formats while retaining its core purpose of enlightening and transforming readers. Books, whether in print or digital form, continue to inspire, educate, and provoke thought.

The enduring importance of literature lies in its ability to adapt and remain pertinent to each generation. While technology has introduced new ways of consuming information, the fundamental power of a well-told story remains unchanged. Literature's ability to evoke emotions, challenge perceptions, and spark meaningful conversations ensures its relevance.

Historical Evolution of Literature

The historical development of literature is a rich tapestry woven with threads from different eras, cultures, and social changes. This section aims to trace the evolution of literature, highlighting how its forms and functions have transformed over time.

Ancient Origins of Literature

Literature has its roots in the oral traditions of ancient civilisations, where stories were passed down through generations by word of mouth. These narratives often explained natural phenomena, taught moral lessons, and preserved a community's history and culture. The earliest written texts include the "Epic of Gilgamesh" from Mesopotamia, ancient Egyptian hieroglyphs, and the Vedas from India. These works demonstrate the early use of literature to preserve knowledge and cultural heritage.

Classical Antiquity

As societies developed writing systems, literature began to flourish in written form. In ancient Greece and Rome, literature reached new heights with the creation of epic poems like Homer's "Iliad" and "Odyssey," as well as Virgil's "Aeneid." These works were not only artistic achievements but also served political and educational purposes. Philosophical texts, such as Plato's dialogues and Aristotle's treatises, further expanded the scope of literature, blending narrative skills with intellectual inquiry (Rexroth, 2018).

The Middle Ages

During the Middle Ages, literature was heavily influenced by religion. Most literary works of this period were produced by monks and clerics and intended to propagate Christian teachings. Notable examples include Dante Alighieri's "The Divine Comedy" and Geoffrey Chaucer's "The Canterbury Tales." These works combined elements of folklore, mythology, and contemporary life to create instructional and entertaining stories.

The Renaissance

The Renaissance marked a revival of interest in the classical ideals of Greece and Rome, leading to an explosion of literary production. William Shakespeare's plays and sonnets, Miguel de Cervantes' "Don Quixote," and Michel de Montaigne's essays exemplify the diverse forms literature took during this period. Johannes Gutenberg's invention of the printing press in the mid-15th century played a crucial role in disseminating these works, making literature accessible to a broader audience.

The Enlightenment

The Enlightenment introduced literature emphasising reason, individualism, and scepticism of traditional authority. Writers like Voltaire, John Locke, and Jean-Jacques Rousseau explored themes of human rights, democracy, and scientific progress. Literary forms during this period included essays, philosophical treatises, and satire, all aimed at questioning established norms and advocating for social reform.

Romanticism

In reaction to the rationalism of the Enlightenment, the Romantic movement emerged, celebrating emotion, nature, and individualism. Poets like William Wordsworth, Samuel Taylor Coleridge, and Lord Byron expressed their admiration for the sublime beauty of nature and the depth of human emotion. Romantic literature often featured heroic protagonists who struggled against societal constraints and explored the complexities of the human psyche.

Realism and Naturalism

The late 19th century saw the rise of Realism and Naturalism, literary movements that sought to depict life accurately and objectively. Authors like Leo Tolstoy, Gustave Flaubert, and Émile Zola focused on everyday experiences and social issues, eschewing the idealism and grandeur of Romantic literature. Their works provided detailed observations of human behaviour and social environments, often critiquing the society they lived in.

Modernism

Modernist literature, emerging in the early 20th century, broke away from traditional forms and experimented with narrative structure, language, and themes. Significant social and technological changes, including the effects of World War I and rapid industrialisation, marked this period. Writers like James Joyce, Virginia Woolf, and T.S. Eliot employed techniques such as stream of consciousness, unreliable narrators, and fragmented narratives to reflect the complexities of modern life (J., 2023).

Postmodernism

Postmodern literature, which gained prominence after World War II, continued the experimental trends of Modernism but with a greater focus on paradox, unreliable narrators, and metafiction. Authors like Thomas Pynchon, Jorge Luis Borges, and Margaret Atwood blurred the boundaries between fiction and reality, often questioning the nature of truth and representation. Postmodern works frequently incorporate pastiches of different styles and genres, reflecting contemporary society's pluralistic and fragmented nature.

Contemporary Literature

Literature continues to evolve in the contemporary era, reflecting the diverse experiences and perspectives of a globalized world. Genres such as graphic novels, digital storytelling, and young adult fiction have gained popularity, expanding the definition of what constitutes literature. Contemporary authors often address themes like identity, migration, and environmental concerns, engaging with the pressing issues of our time.

Distinguishing Between Fiction and Non-Fiction

To fully understand literature, it's essential to differentiate between fiction and nonfiction, two primary categories that serve distinct purposes in the literary world. Fiction and nonfiction have unique characteristics that cater to readers' needs and interests.

Fiction involves imaginative storytelling where the author creates characters, settings, events, and narratives that do not exist in reality. These stories often aim to entertain, offering readers an escape from the mundane or a way to explore complex human emotions and hypothetical scenarios. Fictional works span a variety of subgenres, including mystery, romance, fantasy, magical realism, thriller, science fiction, crime, and horror. Each subgenre has its own set of conventions and tropes. For instance, mysteries often revolve around a detective solving a crime, while fantasy includes elements of magic and otherworldly beings.

One classic example of fiction is Mary Shelley's "Frankenstein," which blends science fiction and horror to explore themes of creation and monstrosity. Another popular work is J.K. Rowling's "Harry Potter" series, which falls under the fantasy genre and captures readers with its magical world and complex characters. Fiction allows writers to stretch the boundaries of the natural world, create new realms, and develop narratives that reflect their artistic vision and creativity.

On the other hand, nonfiction refers to works that relay accurate, verifiable information about real people, places, events, and concepts. The primary goal of nonfiction is to educate, inform, or document actual occurrences. This category includes memoirs, biographies, essays, articles, scientific papers, textbooks, travelogues, self-help books, and more. Nonfiction is committed to truth and factual accuracy, making it a reliable source of knowledge and information for readers.

For example, Laura Hillenbrand's biography "Unbroken" provides a detailed account of Louis Zamperini's life, focusing on his experiences as an Olympic athlete and a World War II POW. Similarly, Yuval Noah Harari's "Sapiens: A Brief History of Humankind" is a historical analysis that educates readers on the evolution of humans over centuries. These works strive to offer insights into real-world issues and phenomena, helping readers develop a deeper understanding of various subjects.

A critical difference between fiction and nonfiction lies in their approach to narrative. Fiction employs a subjective, interpretive style, allowing for artistic freedom and emotional engagement. Authors use literary devices such as symbolism, foreshadowing, and metaphors to build compelling stories. In contrast, nonfiction focuses on objectivity and reliability, presenting facts and evidence to support its claims.

While nonfiction can utilise narrative techniques to make the content more engaging, it must remain faithful to the factual content.

The purpose of fiction and nonfiction also diverges significantly. Fiction aims to entertain, provoke thought, and evoke emotions by presenting imaginary scenarios, whereas nonfiction seeks to educate, inform, and persuade based on real-life situations. Readers turn to fiction for creative escapism and to explore different perspectives on life, while they look to nonfiction for practical knowledge, intellectual growth, and a deeper appreciation of reality.

Moreover, the scope of fiction and nonfiction extends to their impact on readers and society. Fiction can influence cultural norms, inspire change, and provide commentary on social issues through allegory and satire. It stimulates empathy by allowing readers to experience lives and circumstances different from their own. Notable examples include George Orwell's "1984," a dystopian novel that critiques totalitarianism, and Harper Lee's "To Kill a Mockingbird," which addresses racial injustice.

Nonfiction plays a crucial role in documenting history, disseminating scientific discoveries, and spreading awareness about critical issues. Works like Rachel Carson's "Silent Spring" have profoundly impacted environmental movements and policy changes. Similarly, educational texts and scholarly articles are foundational for academic advancement and professional development.

Despite their differences, fiction and nonfiction share some similarities. Both genres require effective writing techniques, engaging language, and a clear purpose to captivate readers. They can convey themes, ideas, and messages that resonate on a personal and societal level. Fiction and nonfiction allow readers to explore diverse perspectives, gain insights into human nature, and expand their understanding of the world.

The Role of the Reader in Interpreting Texts

In traditional views of literature, readers were often seen as passive recipients, absorbing the messages and artistic elements conveyed by authors. This perspective, however, has shifted significantly in contemporary literary theory, which now emphasises the active role of readers in shaping meaning and interpretation. This shift highlights that reading is not a one-way transaction but an interactive process in which readers bring their own experiences, emotions, and perspectives to bear on the text.

Reader-response theory is pivotal in understanding this interactive dynamic. It posits that a literary work does not exist independently of its audience but comes alive through reading. The reader's interpretation and emotional responses are integral to the meaning of the text. Literature becomes a collaborative creation where the author provides the text, and the reader imbues it with significance based on their unique background and life experiences (Long, 2024).

For example, consider a classic text like Jane Austen's Pride and Prejudice. A reader in the 19th century might focus primarily on the romantic plot and social commentary reflective of their time. However, a modern reader may interpret the exact text in light of contemporary issues such as gender roles and class dynamics, bringing a new layer of meaning to Austen's work. This interpretation variability underscores readers' active role in the literary experience.

Active engagement with texts involves several vital practices. Firstly, readers should approach a text with an open mind, ready to explore different avenues of meaning. This requires close reading—a careful and detailed analysis of the text's language, structure, and themes. By engaging deeply with the text, readers uncover layers of meaning that might not be immediately apparent. For instance, in William Faulkner's "The Sound and the Fury," the fragmented narrative and complex chronology demand an attentive reader who can piece together the story's intricate puzzle.

Secondly, reflecting on personal experiences is crucial for active engagement. Readers should consider how their own life experiences intersect with the themes and characters in the text. This reflective practice allows readers to form a more personal connection with the text, making the reading experience both enriching and transformative. For instance, a reader who has experienced loss may find new resonance in the themes of grief and memory in Gabriel Garcia Marquez's "One Hundred Years of Solitude."

Furthermore, readers must recognise that their interpretations are flexible and dynamic. The meaning of a text can evolve with each reading, influenced by the reader's changing perspectives and circumstances. This fluidity is a core aspect of subjective reader response, suggesting that the exact text can yield different meanings at different times in a reader's life. As Umberto Eco observes, the interaction between reader and text is dynamic, involving intellectual, emotional, and physical dimensions (Sandoval, 2023).

Eco's concept of 'openness' highlights this interactive nature, indicating that texts invite multiple interpretations while providing a framework. For instance, his novel "The Name of the Rose" offers a historical mystery that can be read in various ways—an intellectual puzzle, a comment on medieval religious politics, or a philosophical reflection on the nature of truth and interpretation. Each reading can bring out different text facets, illustrating how reader engagement shapes literary meaning.

Guidelines for active reading can help foster this dynamic interaction. They include:

1. **Annotate the Text**: Make notes, highlight passages, and jot down questions or reactions as you read. This keeps you engaged and helps track your thought process.
2. **Discuss with Others**: Sharing interpretations and insights with fellow readers can broaden your perspective and deepen your understanding of the text.
3. **Revisit the Text**: Reading a text multiple times can reveal new meanings and connections that were missed initially.
4. **Relate to Other Works**: Compare and contrast the text with other literary works, considering thematic similarities, stylistic differences, and historical contexts. This intertextual approach enriches your overall comprehension.

By actively engaging with texts through these methods, readers move beyond passive consumption and become co-creators of meaning. This participatory role enhances their appreciation of literature, making it a more interactive and personal experience.

Moreover, recognising the transformative potential of reading is essential. Engaging deeply with diverse texts can challenge preconceived notions and broaden one's worldview. Literature allows readers to encounter different cultures, perspectives, and experiences, fostering empathy and critical thinking. For instance, reading novels by authors from marginalised communities can offer insights into the struggles and triumphs of people whose lives may differ vastly from one's own.

Additionally, literature can catalyse personal growth and self-reflection. Characters' journeys and challenges can mirror the reader's life, offering lessons and inspiration. For example, the resilience and determination of characters in Toni Morrison's works can inspire readers to navigate their adversities with strength and grace.

In educational settings, encouraging students to embrace their active role in literary interpretation can cultivate critical analysis skills and a lifelong love for reading. Educators can facilitate discussions that prompt students to share their interpretations and engage with the text more deeply. By validating students' unique perspectives, educators help them understand that their voices matter in the literary dialogue.

Summary and Reflections

The chapter has delved into various genres and forms that constitute literature, from fiction to nonfiction and poetry to drama. It has outlined the importance of understanding these different categories for a more nuanced appreciation of literary works. By exploring each genre's various characteristics and purposes, readers gain insights into how they shape narratives and convey distinct messages. This knowledge equips students with the tools needed to analyse texts critically, recognising the diversity and richness inherent in literature.

Additionally, the chapter highlighted literature's crucial role in society, serving as both a mirror and a mould for cultural values, social progress, and personal growth. Literature preserves historical contexts, fosters empathy, challenges societal norms, and inspires change. By emphasising readers' active engagement in interpreting texts, the chapter underscores the collaborative nature of meaning-making in literature. This foundational understanding prepares students, adult learners, and educators to engage deeply with literary studies, enhancing their interpretive skills and fostering a lifelong appreciation for the written word.

Reference List

Œ, A. (2023, March 8). *The Power of Literature: How it Shapes Society and Culture.* ILLUMINATION. https://medium.com/illumination/the-power-of-literature-how-it-shapes-society-and-culture-28dc42f04222

Austin, S. (2022, October 27). *The Importance of Literature in Modern Society.* Findcourses.co.uk; findcourses.co.uk. https://www.findcourses.co.uk/inspiration/hobby-fun-leisure-articles/the-importance-of-literature-in-modern-society-17411

Difference Between Fiction and Nonfiction: Know the Differences. (n.d.). Testbook. https://testbook.com/key-differences/difference-between-fiction-and-nonfiction

J., A. (2023, January 23). *Modernism in Literature.* Essaypro.com. https://essaypro.com/blog/modernism-in-literature

Konya, K. (2023, October 4). *Fiction vs. Nonfiction: Definitions and Examples.* What Is the Difference between Fiction and Nonfiction? | Grammarly. https://www.grammarly.com/blog/fiction-vs-nonfiction/

Long, L. (2024). *What Is Reader Response?* Cwi.pressbooks.pub. https://cwi.pressbooks.pub/lit-crit/chapter/what-is-reader-response/

Rexroth, K. (2018, June 28). *literature | Definition, Scope, Types, & Facts.* Encyclopædia Britannica. https://www.britannica.com/art/literature

SuperSummary . (n.d.). SuperSummary. https://www.supersummary.com/genre-in-literature-definition-examples/

Sandoval, D. (2023, September 24). *Literary Theory 101: Umberto Eco's Influence on Reader*

Response Criticism. Arcadia; Arcadia. https://www.byarcadia.org/post/literary-theory-101-umberto-eco-s-influence-on-reader-response-criticism

What Are Literary Genres? (Plus 16 Types To Try) . (n.d.). Indeed Career Guide. https://www.indeed.com/career-advice/career-development/literary-genres

CHAPTER TWO

EXPLORING LITERARY GENRES

"Exploring literary genres opens up a world of diverse storytelling forms, each with unique appeal and characteristics. Understanding these genres is crucial for anyone studying literature, as it provides the tools to appreciate and analyse the vast array of narratives written throughout history. By delving into the distinct features that define each genre, students can develop a deeper appreciation for how authors use different styles and techniques to convey their ideas and engage their readers."

This chapter will provide an overview of various literary genres, including narrative fiction, poetry, drama, and cross-genre literature. Each section will examine the key elements characterising these genres, such as plot structure, characterisation, setting, themes, imagery, sound devices, and more.

Furthermore, the chapter will explore how these components combine to create compelling stories and evoke emotional responses from readers. By understanding the defining traits of each genre, students will be better equipped to recognise and analyse the diverse forms of literature they encounter, enhancing their critical analysis skills and enriching their overall literary experience.

Elements of Narrative Fiction

Understanding and analysing narrative fiction is fundamental for students pursuing literature or related fields. This section will introduce the key elements that define narrative fiction, facilitating the ability to recognise and understand story structures.

Plot

The plot is the sequence of events that make up a story. It includes various elements such as exposition, rising action, climax, falling action, and resolution. These elements collectively form the backbone of the narrative, guiding readers through the characters' journeys and the unfolding of events. For instance, in J.K. Rowling's "Harry Potter" series, the plot follows Harry's growth from a young boy discovering his wizarding heritage to a hero confronting and overcoming various challenges.

There are different types of plots, such as linear, where events unfold chronologically, and non-linear, where the narrative includes flashbacks or shifts in time. Understanding these variations helps appreciate storytelling techniques and how they engage readers. For example, in Gabriel Garcia Marquez's "One Hundred Years of Solitude," the non-linear plot creates a sense of magical realism, enhancing the reader's experience of the fictional world.

Characterisation

Characterisation is the development and portrayal of characters within a narrative. It plays a crucial role in understanding the characters' motivations, behaviours, and transformations throughout the story. Characters can be dynamic, undergoing significant changes, or static, remaining relatively unchanged. In F. Scott Fitzgerald's "The Great Gatsby," Jay Gatsby is a dynamic character whose tragic flaw and relentless pursuit of an unattainable dream lead to his downfall.

Characters can also be round, displaying complex personalities and traits, or flat, serving specific roles with little depth. For example, Sherlock Holmes in Arthur Conan Doyle's detective stories is a round character known for his sharp wit and detailed observation skills. At the same time, Dr. Watson, though necessary, serves more as a flat character who complements Holmes' brilliance.

Effective characterization involves direct methods, such as explicit descriptions by the narrator, and indirect methods, like dialogue and actions that reveal a character's personality. Techniques like internal monologue or stream of consciousness, as seen in James Joyce's Ulysses, allow readers to delve deeper into characters' minds, offering a richer understanding of their psychological states.

Setting

The setting encompasses the time and place where the story unfolds. It significantly influences the mood, context, and events of the narrative. The physical environment, historical period, and cultural backdrop shape the characters' experiences and actions. For instance, the dystopian setting of George Orwell's "1984" creates a bleak and oppressive atmosphere that reflects the totalitarian regime's impact on society and individual freedom.

Settings can be real or imagined, but they must suit the story's themes and add to its believability. In J.R.R. Tolkien's "The Lord of the Rings," the richly detailed world of Middle-earth becomes almost a character, enriching the epic tale with its diverse landscapes, cultures, and histories.

A practical setting provides more than a backdrop; it enhances the narrative's emotional tone and reveals insights into the characters. For example, the moors in Emily Brontë's "Wuthering Heights" symbolise the characters' wild, untamed passions, connecting the environment and the narrative's emotional core.

Theme

Themes are the underlying ideas, beliefs, morals, lessons, or insights the narrative presents. They represent the central arguments that the author wishes to convey and often address universal human experiences and societal issues. Recognising themes helps students connect narratives to broader contexts and personal experiences.

In Harper Lee's "To Kill a Mockingbird," themes of racial injustice, moral growth, and empathy are woven throughout the narrative, prompting readers to reflect on these critical social issues. Similarly, in George Orwell's "Animal Farm," the theme of power and corruption critiques political systems and human nature.

Themes can be explicit, directly stated within the narrative, or implicit, requiring readers to infer them from the story's events, characters, and symbols. The latter approach encourages deeper engagement and analysis. For instance, in Mary Shelley's "Frankenstein," the theme of playing God and the consequences of scientific ambition is not overtly stated but emerges through Victor Frankenstein's tragic quest and its repercussions.

Conclusion Characteristics of Poetry

Poetry is a unique and expressive form of literature that offers rich opportunities for analysis and appreciation. To appreciate poetry, it's essential to understand its distinct features, including imagery, sound devices, form and structure, and emotion and tone.

Imagery plays a crucial role in poetry, creating vivid pictures in the reader's mind and evoking emotional responses. Using descriptive language, poets paint scenes and construct intricate landscapes within just a few lines. For instance, consider Robert Frost's "Stopping by Woods on a Snowy Evening." The imagery of "woods filling up with snow" and "frozen lake" transports readers into a serene, wintry scene. Such detailed images make the poem more engaging and help convey deeper meanings and emotions. By closely examining the imagery in a poem, readers can unlock layers of interpretation and feel a stronger connection to the text.

Sound devices are another critical feature of poetry that enhances its overall effect. Elements like alliteration, assonance, consonance, and onomatopoeia contribute to the poem's musicality and rhythm. Alliteration, the repetition of consonant sounds at the beginning of words, can create a sense of rhythm and focus. For example, in Samuel Taylor Coleridge's "The Rime of the Ancient

Mariner," the line "The fair breeze blew, the white foam flew" uses alliteration to mimic the sea's gentle, rhythmic ebb and flow. Assonance, the repetition of vowel sounds, creates internal rhyming within lines, contributing to the poem's lyrical quality. Consonance, the repetition of consonant sounds within or at the end of words, adds texture to the reading experience. Onomatopoeia, where words imitate natural sounds, can enhance the sensory experience. In Edgar Allan Poe's "The Bells," the repeated use of "tinkle, tinkle, tinkle" mimics the actual sound of bells.

Understanding these sound devices allows readers to appreciate the auditory elements of a poem, enriching their overall experience.

Form and structure are fundamental aspects of poetry that shape its meaning and impact. Different forms follow specific structures, such as sonnets, haikus, odes, and free verse. Sonnets, for example, typically consist of 14 lines with a set rhyme scheme and are often used to explore themes of love and admiration. William Shakespeare's sonnets are famous examples, following an ABABCDCDEFEFGG rhyme scheme.

Haikus, originating from Japan, are three-line poems with a syllable pattern 5-7-5, often focusing on nature. Matsuo Basho's haiku, "An old silent pond... A frog jumps into the pond—Splash! Silence again," captures a moment in nature with brevity and clarity. Odes are formal, often lengthy poems that praise people, events, or objects, while free verse poems lack a fixed metrical pattern, allowing poets greater freedom in expression. Walt Whitman's "Leaves of Grass" exemplifies free verse, using varied line lengths and rhythms to convey his thoughts on life, democracy, and nature. Recognising these forms enables students to analyse poetic styles and their effects, providing insights into the poet's intent and technique.

Emotion and tone are critical for interpreting a poem's message. The tone refers to the poet's attitude toward the subject, ranging from joyful and celebratory to sombre and reflective. For instance, in Maya Angelou's "Still I Rise," the defiant and triumphant tone underscores the speaker's resilience against oppression: "You may shoot me with your words, You may cut me with your eyes, You may kill me with your hatefulness, But still, like air, I'll rise." In contrast, the melancholic tone in W.H. Auden's "Funeral Blues" conveys deep sorrow and loss: "Stop all the clocks, cut off the telephone, Prevent the dog from barking with a juicy bone." Understanding the tone helps readers grasp the emotional undertones of a poem, enhancing their interpretative skills.

Analysing the speaker's perspective further aids in understanding tone and mood. Often, the poet is not the speaker; the narrator may be an imagined character whose viewpoint shapes the poem's tone. In Robert Browning's dramatic monologue "My Last Duchess," the Duke's controlling and jealous nature is revealed through his speech about his deceased wife: "That's my last Duchess painted on the wall, Looking as if she were alive." This exploration of the speaker's role helps readers decode the subtleties of tone and mood, offering a deeper comprehension of the poem's emotional landscape.

Figurative language and poetic devices are central to conveying complex ideas and emotions in poetry.

Metaphors and similes create connections between disparate concepts, adding layers of meaning. For instance, in Sylvia Plath's "Metaphors," the line "I'm a riddle in nine syllables" uses metaphor to describe pregnancy.

Personification imbues inanimate objects with human qualities, enhancing relatability. Emily Dickinson's "Because I Could Not Stop for Death" personifies death as a courteous suitor, transforming the abstract concept into a tangible character. Hyperbole, or exaggerated statements, emphasises particular points, as seen in Andrew Marvell's "To His Coy Mistress": "Love you ten years before the Flood, And you should, if you please, refuse / Till the conversion of the Jews." Irony, where expectations differ from reality, can add a layer of complexity, making readers ponder the underlying messages. These devices enrich the text, prompting multiple interpretations and deeper engagement.

Structure and Elements of Drama

Drama is a unique and vibrant literary genre that offers a dynamic mix of elements that set it apart from other narrative forms. Recognizing and understanding these components is essential for students who wish to engage critically with plays. This subpoint outlines the crucial elements of drama, including plot structure, characters and dialogue, stage directions, and themes. Students can better appreciate and analyse dramatic works by delving into these aspects.

One of the most defining aspects of drama is its plot structure, which often contrasts sharply with narrative structures found in novels or short stories. While dramatic and narrative plots follow a general arc of exposition, rising action, climax, falling action, and resolution, dramas emphasise conflict and tension more intensely. For example, in many plays, the climax occurs just before the final act, creating high suspense. The impact of this structure is evident in Shakespeare's "Hamlet," where the protagonist's indecision drives the plot forward until the final, tragic resolution. Understanding these differences helps students appreciate how drama uniquely builds and resolves tension.

Characters and dialogue are central to how drama unfolds on stage. Unlike narrative fiction, where internal monologues can reveal characters' thoughts and emotions, drama relies heavily on dialogue to convey these aspects. In Arthur Miller's "The Crucible," characters' personalities, motives, and conflicts are revealed through spoken words and interactions. John Proctor's confrontations with other characters expose his inner turmoil and moral struggles, driving the play's central conflict. Thus, analysing dialogue in drama can provide insights into character development and thematic elements.

Stage directions offer another layer of understanding for dramatic works. These instructions guide actors on movement, emotion, and the physical setting, shaping the audience's experience. Stage directions are vital for interpreting and bringing the playwright's vision to life. For instance, Tennessee Williams' "A Streetcar Named Desire" includes detailed stage directions that create a vivid, sensory-rich environment. The description of Blanche DuBois' delicate presence contrasts sharply with Stanley Kowalski's raw energy, underscoring the play's tension. Students can appreciate the nuanced ways stage directions contribute to the storytelling by paying attention to these cues.

Themes in drama often emerge differently than in narrative forms, shaped by the immediacy of performance and the interplay between characters and plot. Dramatic themes tend to be more implicit, revealed through the actions and dialogues of the characters rather than explicitly stated. For example, in Lorraine Hansberry's "A Raisin in the Sun," racial discrimination, family unity, and the American Dream are woven into the characters' struggles and aspirations. The Butler family's experiences reflect broader societal issues, making the themes resonate powerfully with the audience. Analysing how themes unfold in drama can deepen students' understanding of the wider social and cultural context.

Essays and Their Forms

Understanding the various types of essays and their structural elements is crucial for developing solid analytical writing skills. This section will explore four primary types of essays: descriptive, expository, analytical, and persuasive. Each type has unique characteristics and demands specific techniques to master.

Descriptive Essays: One of the most common forms of essay writing, descriptive essays are intended to paint a vivid picture in the reader's mind. This involves using sensory language—words that appeal to the five senses (sight, sound, smell, taste, touch)—to create engaging narratives. For instance, describing a bustling city street should go beyond noting that it's crowded. Instead, one might include the cacophony of car horns, the scent of street food wafting through the air, and the chaotic blend of colours from shop signs and advertisements. By doing so, students learn to transform simple descriptions into immersive experiences for their readers. To craft an adequate descriptive essay, it's essential to focus on detail and make judicious use of figurative language, such as similes and metaphors, which can enhance the imagery.

Expository Essays: These essays serve the purpose of explaining a topic clearly and straightforwardly. Unlike narrative or descriptive essays, expository essays emphasise clarity and structure. They require students to investigate an idea, evaluate evidence, and expound on the subject by offering clear arguments and explanations. A well-structured expository essay typically includes an introduction with a clear thesis statement, several body paragraphs, each supporting a specific point, and a conclusion that succinctly wraps up the discussion. An example would be writing about the effects of global warming: introducing the topic, explaining the causes, detailing its impacts on the environment, and concluding with possible solutions or preventive measures. Students who master expository writing are adept at making logical arguments and organising information.

Analytical Essays: The main objective of an analytical essay is to analyse a given piece of literature, an event, or a concept. Students must present their analysis and provide substantial evidence to support their viewpoints. The thesis statement is central to an analytical essay, which conveys the writer's position on the subject. With a clear thesis, each essay paragraph should focus on a single aspect of the analysis, supported by evidence from relevant sources. For instance, one might examine how the author uses symbolism to convey broader themes in analysing a novel. The student would need to identify specific symbols within the text, interpret their meanings, and connect these interpretations back to the overall thesis. Students learn to develop a coherent argument and critically engage with various texts by doing so.

Persuasive Essays: These essays aim to convince the reader of a particular stance or viewpoint. Effective persuasive writing requires understanding and utilising rhetorical appeals: ethos, pathos, and logos. Ethos appeals to credibility and ethics, establishing the writer's authority. Pathos appeals to emotions, attempting to elicit feelings from the audience. Logos appeals to logic and reason, using facts, statistics, and rational arguments to persuade the reader. Imagine writing a persuasive essay on the importance of renewable energy. To be convincing, one would establish credibility by citing experts in the field (ethos), evoke concern about environmental degradation (pathos), and present precise data on the benefits and feasibility of renewable energy sources (logos). Understanding these rhetorical strategies helps students build stronger arguments and become more effective communicators.

To further elucidate these essay types, let's delve into more practical guidelines and examples:

For **descriptive essays**, begin by selecting a vivid topic. Then, list out the sensory details you want to cover. Use varied sentence structures to maintain reader interest. Incorporating personal anecdotes can also deepen the connection between the reader and the narrative. For example, if describing a childhood memory, recounting the smell of freshly baked cookies, the warmth of the kitchen, and the clinking of family members' laughter can bring the scene to life.

When tackling **expository essays, start with thorough research and organise** your findings logically. An outline can be invaluable here, helping you map out each section of your essay. Every paragraph should transition smoothly to the next, maintaining coherence. Let's say you're writing about the water cycle. Begin with an introduction to its importance, move through stages like evaporation and condensation, and conclude by discussing its significance to ecosystems and human life.

In **analytical essays**, it's essential to dissect the topic comprehensively. Direct quotes from texts can bolster your arguments, provided they are analysed rather than just presented. Keep your analysis focused, always linking it back to your thesis statement. For instance, when examining a historical event, break down its causes, the key players involved, and the short- and long-term impacts, ensuring each segment ties back to your central thesis.

Persuasive essays benefit significantly from thorough audience analysis. Understand their biases and preferences. Tailor your arguments to address these effectively. Use real-world examples to ground your points. If arguing favour school uniforms, highlight studies showing improved student behaviour and performance. Counter potential objections with solid counterarguments.

Cross-genre Experimentation

Cross-genre literature, or genre-blending or hybrid literature, represents the fluidity of literary definitions and challenges traditional boundaries within genres. This subpoint aims to engage students with blending genres, emphasising creativity and innovation in literature.

To begin with, defining cross-genre is essential for understanding its significance. Cross-genre works integrate elements from multiple literary genres, creating a seamless narrative that defies easy classification. These works often include characteristics from different genres, such as the suspense of a thriller combined with the poetic prose of literary fiction or science fiction elements interwoven with mystery. This approach allows authors to transcend conventional storytelling methods, providing readers with a richer, more complex tapestry of themes, settings, and characters.

Examining notable examples of cross-genre texts can illustrate how successful this literary method can be. One prominent example is Margaret Atwood's novel "The Handmaid's Tale," which merges dystopian science fiction with social commentary and feminist literature. Another example is Neil Gaiman's "American Gods," where elements of mythology, fantasy, and contemporary fiction intertwine to create a unique narrative structure. In both cases, these authors skillfully blend genres to offer new perspectives and thought-provoking narratives that challenge readers' expectations.

Furthermore, exploring the impact of genre blending on reader engagement reveals its significance.

Readers today have diverse tastes and are often drawn to stories that break away from traditional genre constraints. By offering a hybrid narrative, authors can pique the interest of a broader audience who seek variety and uniqueness in their reading experiences. Genre blending can influence reader interpretations and expectations, encouraging audiences to think beyond standard genre conventions and embrace multifaceted storylines with unexpected twists.

The role of innovation in cross-genre literature cannot be overstated. Artistic freedom within literature is vital in fostering creativity and pushing the boundaries of traditional storytelling. Authors who experiment with hybrid writing styles have the opportunity to craft innovative narratives that stand out in a crowded literary landscape. For instance, cross-genre writing enables authors to explore themes and topics that may not fit neatly into one category, allowing for a more authentic representation of diverse human experiences. This freedom to innovate often leads to groundbreaking works that resonate deeply with readers and contribute to the evolution of literary traditions.

Moreover, embracing cross-genre writing aligns with changing market trends. The literary market has shown increasing interest in stories that defy genre norms, driven by publishers and readers seeking fresh and compelling content. As a result, cross-genre novels have gained popularity, highlighting the growing appeal of hybrid stories. This trend reflects a shift in reader preferences towards complex, multi-layered narratives that mirror real life's intricacies.

Additionally, cross-genre literature caters to modern readers' desire for complexity and depth. Influenced by a digital age of content consumption, contemporary audiences crave narratives beyond predictable plots and formulaic structures. Hybrid writing allows authors to delve into intricate themes and develop multidimensional characters, offering a more immersive and satisfying reading experience. This complexity can make stories more relatable and engaging as readers connect with the nuanced portrayal of emotions, relationships, and conflicts.

One notable aspect of cross-genre literature is its ability to challenge and redefine traditional genre boundaries. Authors can create narratives that defy easy categorisation by blending elements from various genres. This approach not only enriches the storytelling process but also reflects the evolving nature of genres themselves. As genres evolve, rigid definitions become less relevant, and cross-genre writing emerges as an innovative response to the dynamic landscape of literature.

Furthermore, the rise of cross-media storytelling has expanded the possibilities for cross-genre literature. With the integration of technology and multimedia platforms, authors can experiment with interactive narratives, multimedia elements, and transmedia storytelling. This expansion beyond traditional genres offers new opportunities for creative expression and audience engagement. Cross-media storytelling, for instance, can incorporate visual, auditory, and interactive components that enhance the overall narrative experience, breaking free from the limitations of niche constraints.

Ultimately, cross-genre literature encourages authors to prioritise creative expression over adherence to traditional genre norms. It allows for a more authentic representation of an author's unique voice and vision, fostering creativity without the limitations imposed by specific genres. This artistic freedom is crucial in producing innovative and diverse literary works that resonate with a global audience. In a globalised world, cross-genre writing appeals to a broader international audience by transcending cultural and genre boundaries, making stories more universally relatable.

Summary and Reflections

This chapter has provided an overview of various literary genres and their defining characteristics, aiming to equip students with the knowledge to identify and analyse different forms of literature. We explored narrative fiction, focusing on elements like plot, characterisation, setting, and theme, which are crucial for understanding story structures. The section on poetry introduced vital features such as imagery, sound devices, form and structure, and tone, emphasising how these elements contribute to the overall impact of a poem. The drama was examined through its unique components, including plot structure, characters and dialogue, stage directions, and themes, highlighting its distinctive approach to storytelling. Lastly, we discussed the different types of essays—descriptive, expository, analytical, and persuasive—each serving a specific purpose in academic writing.

By delving into these diverse literary forms, students can develop a deeper appreciation for the richness and complexity of literature. This foundation will help them engage more critically with texts, enhance their analytical skills, and apply these insights in their studies and beyond. Understanding the nuances of different genres allows readers to recognise authors' artistic choices and how these choices shape meaning and experience. As students continue their journey through the world of literature, the knowledge gained from this chapter will serve as a valuable tool for their academic and personal growth.

Reference List

Aria, N. (2023, December 6). *Hybrid Writing: A Blueprint for Crafting Dynamic Novels*. Neda Aria ; Neda Aria . https://www.nedaaria.info/post/hybrid-writing-a-blueprint-for-crafting-dynamic-novels

Crowe, A. (2022, January 31). *What Are the Key Elements of a Story?* Www.prodigygame.com. https://www.prodigygame.com/main-en/blog/story-elements/

Cash, J. (2014). *Dramatic Elements*. The Drama Teacher. https://thedramateacher.com/dramatic-elements/

Das Gupta, S. (2022, April 9). *10 Important Elements of Poetry*. Poem Analysis. https://poemanalysis.com/poetry-explained/elements-of-poetry/

Elements of Drama and Stage Directions - English 10 Study Guide 2024 | Fiveable. (2024). Fiveable. me. https://library.fiveable.me/english-10/unit-5/elements-drama-stage-directions/study-guide/pbZQzRWESTP2Mjso

Golden, S. (2018, February 15). *Cross Genre – The Fictorians*. Fictorians.com. https://www.fictorians.com/category/writing-life/genres/cross-genre/

MasterClass. (2024). *Poetry 101: Learn about poetry, different types of poems, and poetic devices with examples*. Retrieved from https://www.masterclass.com/articles/poetry-101-learn-about-poetry-different-types-of-poems-and-poetic-devices-with-examples

dreamerswriting. (2018, May 11). *Elements of a Story Explained*. Dreamers Creative Writing. https://www.dreamerswriting.com/elements-of-a-story/

CHAPTER THREE

CLASSICAL LITERATURE

"Classical literature forms the cornerstone of Western literary traditions, tracing its roots to ancient Greek and Roman works. This chapter delves into the profound impact of these classical texts, highlighting how they have shaped narrative structures, themes, and character archetypes still prevalent in contemporary storytelling. By exploring Greek epic poetry and tragedies, we uncover foundational elements such as heroism, fate, and human suffering, which continue to resonate across time. Homer's "Iliad" and "Odyssey" narratives provide timeless insights into human nature and the complexities of divine intervention, setting the stage for an enduring literary legacy."

In this chapter, we will examine the prominent characteristics of Greek epic poetry and tragedy, focusing mainly on the works of Homer, Sophocles, and Euripides. We will explore how Greek tragedies use dramatic flaws and societal issues to evoke catharsis, offering moral lessons that transcend their historical context. The role of the chorus in Greek tragedies and its function as a bridge between the narrative and the audience will also be covered. Furthermore, we will discuss Hesiod's "Theogony" and its contribution to understanding ancient Greek cosmology and theology. Additionally, the chapter will highlight the educational importance of epic poetry in ancient Greece and its influence on rhetoric and oratory skills. Ultimately, this exploration aims to demonstrate how classical literature reflects the historical and societal contexts from which it emerged, enriching our understanding of contemporary literary practices.

Greek Epic Poetry and Tragedy

Exploring the characteristics and significance of Greek epic poetry and tragedies reveals their enduring impact on narrative structures and literary themes. Central to this exploration are Homer's "Iliad" and "Odyssey." These monumental works establish foundational themes such as heroism, fate, and human suffering. The "Iliad," depicting the Trojan War, offers a profound insight into heroic virtue and the inevitability of fate. Achilles, the central character, epitomises the ancient Greek ideal of heroism, yet his journey also underscores human vulnerabilities and the tragic consequences of rage.

In the "Odyssey," readers encounter another layer of heroism through Odysseus's arduous journey home after the fall of Troy. His adventures emphasise intelligence, cunning, and perseverance, setting standards for character development that continue to influence modern narratives. The interaction between gods and mortals throughout these epics adds complexity to the narrative, portraying divine intervention as a source of aid and a harbinger of suffering. This interplay captures the essence of human experience—how forces beyond our control shape our destiny, a theme still resonant in contemporary storytelling.

Greek tragedies further delve into human nature by conveying moral lessons through dramatised flaws and societal issues. Playwrights like Sophocles and Euripides masterfully use tragedy to evoke catharsis, an emotional purging that leaves the audience with relief and insight. In Sophocles' "Oedipus Rex," the protagonist's quest for truth leads to self-discovery and inevitable downfall, illustrating the Greek belief in unavoidable fate and the tragic consequences of human hubris. Meanwhile, Euripides' "Medea" explores themes of revenge, passion, and the position of women in society, offering a powerful commentary on human flaws and societal expectations.

The chorus in Greek tragedies is crucial in bridging the narrative and the audience. Acting as a commentator, the chorus reflects on the unfolding events, often influencing the narrative pacing and enhancing emotional engagement. By voicing collective thoughts and societal values, the chorus serves as a moral compass, guiding the audience through complex plot developments and accentuating the thematic depth of the plays. This element of Greek tragedies allows viewers to connect more deeply with the character's struggles and the overarching moral messages.

Mythological references throughout Greek epics and tragedies enrich the storytelling, connecting cultural values with mythic narratives. These references provide historical and religious context and explore human experiences and societal norms. In Homer's works, mythological allusions deepen the narrative by linking individual quests to more significant, timeless stories. For instance, the recurrent mention of the gods reflects the Greeks' understanding of human life as intertwined with divine will, creating a rich tapestry that mirrors real human experiences.

Moreover, Hesiod's "Theogony" is a prime example of Greek epic poetry that delves into the origins of the gods and the universe. This work offers invaluable insights into ancient Greek cosmology and theology, presenting cosmogonic myths that explain the world's creation and the genealogies of deities. The grand themes of heroism, divine interaction, and mythological events found in "Theogony" further illustrate these narratives' deep-seated cultural significance. Through vivid imagery and structured poetic elements, Hesiod's work reinforces the didactic purpose of Greek poetry, emphasising moral and ethical lessons integral to ancient Greek culture (Greek Epic Poetry: Characteristics & Themes | Vaia, 2019).

Adding to the educational value of these texts, epic poetry played a vital role in the ancient Greek educational system. Students learned rhetoric and oratory skills by studying these lengthy poems, which is essential to a well-rounded education. Epic poetry's intricate structure and vivid imagery gave young learners examples of persuasive storytelling and effective communication, skills highly regarded in Greek society. Thus, Greek epic poetry was not just a form of entertainment but a means to impart critical thinking and eloquence, impacting the intellectual development of students.

In addition to their literary importance, Greek epics and tragedies reflect the historical and societal contexts from which they emerged. These works chronicle historical and mythological events, repositories of collective memory and cultural identity. The themes and stories in these poems and plays reflect the values and beliefs of ancient Greek society, reinforcing notions of honour, bravery, and ethical conduct. They also highlight the Greeks' understanding of their gods, perceived as powerful yet capricious entities influencing human destiny.

The artistic merit of Greek epic poetry lies not only in its thematic richness but also in its formal composition. Typically written in dactylic hexameter, the length and meter create a rhythmic quality that aids memorisation and oral recitation. Poets like Homer used repetitive epithets and formulaic language to maintain the poem's rhythm and meter, facilitating the oral tradition in which these works were first performed (Greek Epic Poetry: Characteristics & Themes | Vaia, 2019). This practice also aided listeners in following the story more efficiently, as familiar descriptions anchored their understanding of the narrative.

Furthermore, Greek literature evolved through various periods, from the Archaic to the Classical and Hellenistic eras, each contributing distinct forms and ideas. During the Archaic period, poetry was intended to be sung or recited, with myths interweaving history and legend. The flexibility of myth allowed poets to express new concepts, advancing Greek thought through refashioned narratives. The Classical period saw the flowering of dramatic arts, with tragedies exploring profound philosophical and ethical questions. The Hellenistic period continued to innovate, blending earlier traditions with contemporary themes and styles (Browning, 2019).

Roman Contributions to Literature

In examining how Roman writers adapted Greek literary forms, it is essential to recognise Greece's profound influence on Roman literature. This adaptation process contributed to the evolution of literature and expanded thematic exploration, paving the way for future literary endeavours.

Virgil's "Aeneid" is a prime example of this cultural synthesis. The epic, written during the Augustan Age, mirrors the structure and style of Homer's "Iliad" and "Odyssey," employing dactylic hexameter and epic conventions familiar to Greek audiences. However, Virgil imbued his work with distinctively Roman ideals of duty, pietas (devotion), and nationalism. The protagonist, Aeneas, is portrayed as a paragon of duty, committed to founding Rome despite personal sacrifices. This narrative intertwines Roman historical destiny with mythological grandeur, thus pioneering character complexity and thematic depth innovations that were less prominent in earlier Greek epics. Additionally, Virgil explores themes of unrequited love and revenge through characters like Dido and Turnus, showcasing an emotional intricacy that reflects Roman cultural values.

Ovid's "Metamorphoses" further illustrates Roman authors' creative use of mythology. This narrative poem comprises fifteen books, weaving together mythological tales centred on transformation. Unlike Greek predecessors who often focused on singular plots, Ovid employed a continuous narrative that highlighted change and fluidity, both thematically and structurally. For instance, the tale of Daphne and Apollo emphasises physical transformation while metaphorically exploring themes of pursuit and escape. Such innovation served as a precursor to later narrative techniques in works ranging from medieval allegories to modernist literature. Ovid's playful wit, vivid imagery, and imaginative storytelling have influenced countless artists and writers, solidifying the enduring legacy of his works in Western literary tradition.

Roman satire, epitomised by authors like Juvenal and Horace, represents another critical dimension of Roman literary innovation. Borrowing from the Greek Old Comedy's penchant for social critique, Roman satirists refined their approach to blending humour with moral commentary. Juvenal's biting satires, for instance, expose the vices and follies of Roman society, targeting corruption, greed, and hypocrisy with caustic wit.

Horace's satires, in contrast, are characterised by a more relaxed tone, blending entertainment with reflective wisdom. His concept of "dulce et utile" (sweet and useful) encapsulates satire's dual purpose: amuse and educate. This balance between entertainment and moral lessons engaged Roman audiences and influenced the development of literary satire, leaving a blueprint for future satirists across cultures and eras.

The impact of Roman rhetoric, mainly through figures like Cicero, extends beyond oratory into literature. Cicero's rhetorical principles significantly influenced narrative persuasion and character development in Roman prose and poetry. His speeches, such as the Catiline Orations, exemplify the power of persuasive rhetoric in conveying complex arguments and swaying public opinion. By mastering techniques like ethos (credibility), pathos (emotional appeal), and logos (logical argument), Cicero demonstrated the intricate relationship between compelling storytelling and rhetorical skills. This interplay enriched Roman narratives, imbuing characters with greater depth and authenticity. For example, in the

"Aeneid," Aeneas' speeches reflect Ciceronian principles, illustrating his leadership and ethical resolve. Thus, Roman rhetoric provided foundational tools for literary expression, enhancing the art of storytelling through persuasive eloquence.

Mythology and Its Impact on Literature

The mythology of ancient cultures forms the bedrock of Western literature, embedding universal themes, narrative frameworks, and character archetypes that continue to resonate in contemporary storytelling. By examining how mythology has shaped these literary elements, we can better understand its enduring influence on narrative construction and thematic exploration.

Firstly, mythology introduces universal themes that have pervaded literature across time and cultures.

Stories of creation, destruction, and rebirth serve as metaphors for human experiences and existential questions. For instance, creation myths often symbolise beginnings, offering insight into humanity's quest to understand the origin of life and the cosmos. The Biblical Genesis story or the Greek myth of Gaia are prime examples. These narratives explore themes of order emerging from chaos, reflecting human fascination with origins and existence. Destruction and rebirth myths, such as the phoenix rising from its ashes or the seasonal death and resurrection of Persephone, address themes of renewal and transformation. Such motifs parallel human growth, loss, and recovery cycles, providing a lens through which readers can process their life experiences and challenges.

Additionally, mythology has given rise to enduring character archetypes that populate stories across genres and eras. The hero, mentor, trickster, and villain archetypes carry deep psychological and symbolic significance. The hero's journey, popularised by Joseph Campbell, follows a quintessential pattern: departure, initiation, and return. Characters like Odysseus, King Arthur, and Harry Potter undertake this journey, symbolising personal growth and the struggle against adversity. Mentors such as Merlin or Gandalf guide heroes, representing wisdom and support. Tricksters like Loki and Puck introduce chaos, challenging societal norms and highlighting the complexities of human behaviour. Villains such as Hades or Darth Vader embody opposition, creating conflict essential for narrative tension. These archetypal characters allow authors to explore the breadth of human experience, making stories relatable and psychologically rich.

Intertextuality, or the interplay between texts, further underscores mythology's impact on literature. Authors draw upon mythological references not just as allusions but as integral components of narrative structure and theme. We uncover layers of literary influence and continuity by comparing classic texts and their mythological roots. For instance, James Joyce's "Ulysses" reinterprets Homer's "Odyssey," setting the ancient epic in modern Dublin. This intertextual dialogue enriches the reading experience, highlighting how contemporary narratives are woven with mythological threads. Mythology, thus, serves as a scaffold upon which new stories are constructed, allowing authors to engage with and reinterpret timeless tales in novel ways.

Modern literature vividly demonstrates the reinterpretation of mythology, addressing contemporary themes like identity, cultural belonging, and social critique. In works like Neil Gaiman's "American Gods," ancient deities find themselves in modern America, struggling for relevance in a rapidly changing world. Here, mythology addresses cultural identity and adaptation questions, reflecting the ongoing human search for meaning in a diverse and evolving society. Similarly, Madeline Miller's "Circe" reimagines the story of the eponymous enchantress from "The Odyssey," focusing on her perspective. This retelling empowers a traditionally marginalised voice, resonating with modern themes of gender, autonomy, and resilience. By revisiting mythological narratives, authors highlight the timeless nature of these stories while simultaneously adapting them to address present-day issues.

Furthermore, mythological themes and archetypes provide a framework for exploring existential and philosophical questions in literature. Myths often pose profound inquiries about fate, destiny, and the nature of good and evil. They challenge characters—and, by extension, readers—to grapple with moral dilemmas and the complexities of human nature. For example, the Greek tragedy of Oedipus explores fate and free will, with Oedipus' attempts to evade prophecy only leading him closer to his destined path. This theme persists in modern works such as George Orwell's "1984," where the characters wrestle with the oppressive inevitability imposed by totalitarian control. The persistent relevance of these themes illustrates mythology's capacity to address fundamental aspects of the human condition.

Educationally, understanding mythology's role in literature equips readers with analytical tools to decode complex narratives. Recognising mythological references and archetypal patterns enhances comprehension and appreciation of literary works. For students and educators alike, this knowledge fosters critical thinking and cultural literacy, enriching the study and teaching of literature. Moreover, mythology offers a shared cultural framework that bridges different societies and epochs, underscoring the universality of specific human experiences and emotions.

Philosophical Writings

Integrating philosophical thought in classical literature shapes narrative structures and thematic depth. This subpoint delves into how philosophies from ancient Greece to the 20th century inform literary compositions, instilling layers of meaning and complexity in the stories we read.

Socratic Dialogue and Plato's Influence

One significant influence on narrative forms is the Socratic dialogue, named after its originator, Socrates. Although primarily employed as a philosophical tool, his method of questioning and dialogue profoundly impacts literary discourse. Socratic dialogues introduce dynamic elements into storytelling by engaging characters in questioning their beliefs and assumptions. Plato, a student of Socrates, harnessed this approach in his writings, creating profound narratives that explore truth and morality. One of the most notable examples is Plato's allegory of the cave in "The Republic." This allegory uses a simple story to convey complex ideas about reality and enlightenment. Through this method, Plato advances philosophical arguments and enriches the narrative with layers of meaning that challenge readers to think deeply about the nature of truth and knowledge.

Aristotle's 'Poetics' and Literary Theory

Aristotle, another towering figure in Greek philosophy, made substantial contributions to literary theory through his work "Poetics." In this treatise, Aristotle formulates foundational concepts such as tragedy, catharsis, and the unity of plot, which have influenced storytelling across centuries. His analysis of tragedy, for instance, emphasises the importance of a coherent plot that evokes pity and fear, leading to a cathartic experience for the audience. He lays down guidelines on how stories should be structured for maximum emotional impact, stressing that each plot element should contribute to the overall coherence and purpose of the narrative. His theories bridge the gap between abstract philosophical concepts and practical storytelling techniques, allowing writers to create narratives that resonate deeply with human emotions and experiences.

Stoic Philosophy in Literature

Stoicism, a school of philosophy founded in the early 3rd century BCE, offers another layer of depth to literature through themes of resilience, virtue, and rationality. Stoic philosophers like Seneca, Epictetus, and Marcus Aurelius emphasised the importance of maintaining inner peace and virtue in adversity. These principles find their way into literature, informing the development of characters who embody stoic virtues. For example, in many narratives, protagonists face immense challenges with unwavering resolve and moral integrity, reflecting Stoic ideals. Integrating these philosophical tenets not only shapes character arcs but also imparts moral lessons, encouraging readers to contemplate the virtues of resilience and ethical conduct in their own lives (Baltzly, 2023).

Existential Themes in Modern Literature

Moving into the 20th century, existentialism emerges as a significant philosophical influence on literature. Existential philosophers like Jean-Paul Sartre and Albert Camus explore themes of meaning, authenticity, and individual freedom, profoundly impacting narrative structures and character development in contemporary literature. Sartre's concept of "existence precedes essence" suggests that individuals must create meaning and purpose in an indifferent universe. This idea manifests in literary works through characters grappling with questions of identity and existential despair. Similarly, Camus' exploration of the absurd—the conflict between humans' search for meaning and the silent, indifferent world— finds expression in narratives that challenge readers to confront existence's inherent uncertainty and ambiguity. These existential themes deepen the characters' psychological complexity and their narratives, prompting readers to reflect on fundamental questions about life, purpose, and the human condition.

Integration and Impact

Integrating these philosophical thoughts into literature adds more than intellectual depth; it also enhances the emotional and ethical dimensions of the narratives. Philosophical concepts provide writers with frameworks to explore questions about human nature, morality, and the universe. By weaving these ideas into their stories, authors can create rich, multifaceted narratives that engage readers on multiple levels.

For instance, consider how the values of questioning and seeking truth, derived from Socratic dialogues, encourage readers to critically evaluate their beliefs and the world around them—characters inspired by Stoic philosophy model resilience and virtuous living, offering moral exemplars to emulate. Meanwhile, existential themes push readers to confront the uncertainties of life, fostering a deeper understanding of the human experience.

Moreover, the interplay between these philosophical ideas and literary forms creates a fertile ground for innovation in storytelling. Writers experiment with narrative structures and character development, drawing inspiration from philosophical doctrines. This experimentation leads to the creation of diverse literary styles and genres, enriching the literary tradition and expanding the possibilities of narrative art.

Conclusion

Examining the profound influence of philosophical thought on classical literature, we uncover the intricate ways in which philosophical ideas shape narrative structures and thematic depth. From the dynamic dialogues of Socrates and Plato's allegories to Aristotle's literary theories and the ethical teachings of Stoicism to the existential musings of modern philosophers, these ideas enhance the complexity and resonance of literary works.

Transmission of Classical Texts

Classical texts' preservation, adaptation, and transformation are integral to our understanding and appreciation of modern literature. Their journey from ancient manuscripts to digital formats highlights the enduring influence of classical works on contemporary literary traditions.

Manuscript culture played a crucial role in the historical preservation of classical works. In ancient times, scribes meticulously copied texts by hand, a labour-intensive process often involving significant challenges. Manuscripts were prone to physical decay and loss, and copying required immense precision to ensure the integrity of the original text. Scribes preserved the words and added annotations and commentaries, which provided valuable insights for future scholars. This process underscored the importance of maintaining and passing knowledge down through generations.

During the medieval period, monasteries became centres of manuscript preservation. Monastic scribes dedicated their lives to transcribing classical texts, ensuring that the wisdom of ancient authors like Homer, Virgil, and Plato was not lost to time. These efforts were not merely acts of copying but were imbued with a reverence for the intellectual heritage they were safeguarding. Such painstaking work illustrates the dedication to historical preservation that allowed classical literature to survive the ravages of time and continue to inspire future generations.

The Renaissance marked a revival of interest in classical knowledge, spearheaded by figures like Petrarch and Erasmus. This period saw a renewed focus on studying ancient texts, leading to the emergence of new literary movements such as Humanism. Petrarch, often considered the father of Humanism, advocated for the return to classical sources, believing that the wisdom of antiquity could illuminate contemporary life. Erasmus furthered this cause by editing and translating Greek and Roman texts, making them more accessible to European scholars.

The Renaissance also witnessed the development of the printing press, a technological innovation that revolutionised the dissemination of written works. The ability to produce multiple copies of a text rapidly expanded the reach of classical literature, allowing it to permeate various aspects of cultural and intellectual life. This period revived classical knowledge and laid the groundwork for its continued relevance in literature and other art forms.

Translations have played a pivotal role in broadening the reach of classical literature. Translators act as cultural mediators, interpreting and adapting ancient texts for new audiences. This process often involves navigating linguistic and cultural differences, leading to varied interpretations and adaptations that reflect the translator's context. For instance, the translations of Homer's "Odyssey" have been influenced by each translator's linguistic and stylistic choices, resulting in different portrayals of the same epic narrative. Translators bring their perspectives to the text, sometimes highlighting themes or elements that resonate with contemporary readers.

Cultural exchanges through translations impact how classical narratives are perceived and appreciated. Translating Greek and Latin classics into vernacular languages during the Renaissance made these works accessible to a broader audience, democratising knowledge. Interpreting these texts through diverse cultural lenses underscores their universal themes, reinforcing their ongoing relevance.

By engaging with classical literature through translation, modern readers can appreciate the timeless nature of these works and their capacity to address fundamental human experiences.

In contemporary times, digitalisation has transformed access to classical texts. Online databases and eBooks facilitate the global dissemination of ancient works, breaking down geographical and economic barriers to knowledge. Digital archives like Project Gutenberg and the Perseus Digital Library offer free access to a vast array of classical literature, enabling students, scholars, and enthusiasts to explore these texts from anywhere in the world. This technological advancement ensures the longevity and accessibility of classical works, allowing them to be reinterpreted and reimagined in new media expressions.

Digital platforms also provide tools for interactive and collaborative engagement with classical literature. Annotations, hyperlinked references, and multimedia resources enrich the reading experience, offering deeper insights into the texts' historical and cultural contexts. These digital innovations highlight the dynamic nature of classical literature, demonstrating its adaptability to modern modes of consumption and study.

The preservation, adaptation, and transformation of classical texts throughout history illustrate their profound impact on modern literature. From the meticulous efforts of scribes in manuscript culture to the Renaissance revival of classical knowledge, the translation of texts across languages and cultures, and the advent of digitalisation, each stage in this journey reflects a commitment to maintaining the relevance of ancient works. By engaging with classical literature, modern readers can draw connections between past and present, recognising the foundational elements that continue to shape contemporary literary traditions.

Summary and Reflections

This chapter has delved into the foundational elements of Western literature by examining ancient Greek epic poetry and tragedies. Through works like Homer's "Iliad" and "Odyssey," we've explored themes such as heroism, fate, and human suffering, observing how these narratives set standards for character development that echo in modern storytelling.

Greek tragedies by playwrights like Sophocles and Euripides reveal deep insights into human nature and societal issues. They use dramatic flaws to evoke emotional responses and moral contemplation.

The importance of mythological references in these ancient texts further enriches their narratives, connecting cultural values with timeless stories.

Whether through the grand cosmology of Hesiod's "Theogony" or the educational role of epic poetry, we've seen how these works reflect historical contexts and reinforce societal norms. This exploration underscores the lasting impact of Greek literature on contemporary literary traditions, providing a profound understanding of how ancient themes and structures continue to shape our narrative landscapes today.

Reference List

Ancient Roman Literature - Art and Literature Study Guide 2024 | Fiveable. (2024). Fiveable. me.

https://library.fiveable.me/art-and-literature/unit-1/ancient-roman-literature/study-guide/MWFOcvyNGcms1rul

Baltzly, D. (2023). *Stoicism (Stanford Encyclopedia of Philosophy)*. Stanford.edu. https://plato.stanford.edu/entries/stoicism/

Browning, R. (2019). *Greek literature*. Encyclopædia Britannica. https://www.britannica.com/art/Greek-literature

DHQ: Digital Humanities Quarterly: Diachronic trends in Homeric translations. (2024). Digitalhumanities.org. http://www.digitalhumanities.org/dhq/vol/11/2/000297/000297.html

Greek Epic Poetry: Characteristics & Themes | Vaia. (2019). Vaia. https://www.vaia.com/en-us/explanations/greek/greek-literature/greek-epic-poetry/

Shukla, B. (2024, February 26). *Mythology in Modern English Literature: Archetypes and Symbols*. Basudew Academic Hub. https://basudewacademichub.in/the-influence-of-mythology-in-modern-literature/

Studies in Manuscript Cultures. (2024). De Gruyter. https://www.degruyter.com/serial/SMC-B/html

Socrates, Plato, and Aristotle: The Big Three of Greek Philosophy. (2021, December 22). Dummies. https://www.dummies.com/article/body-mind-spirit/philosophy/philosophers/socrates-plato-and-aristotle-the-big-three-in-greek-philosophy-199341/

Wasson, D. (2017, September 27). *Roman Literature*. World History Encyclopedia. https://www.worldhistory.org/Roman_Literature/

amoyaan. (2015, July 2). *The Power of Storytelling and Mythology*. The Dreamlight Fugitive.

https://dreamlightfugitive.wordpress.com/2015/07/02/
the-power-of-storytelling-and-mythology/

57

CHAPTER FOUR

MEDIEVAL AND RENAISSANCE LITERATURE

"*Medieval and Renaissance literature marks a pivotal transition in the history of written works. This period saw the evolution from a focus on chivalric romances, with their tales of knightly valour, moral quests, and allegorical narratives, to the rich humanistic themes of the Renaissance. The Renaissance literature is characterized by a profound exploration of individual experience and personal choice, a stark contrast to the collective themes of the medieval era. By examining the distinct characteristics and societal influences that shaped these epochs, readers will gain a deeper understanding of how literature reflected and influenced the cultural contexts of the times.*"

This chapter provides a comprehensive exploration of the elements of medieval chivalric romances, delving into how these tales encapsulated the values of honour, bravery, and courtly love prevalent during the Middle Ages. The chapter also highlights significant authors and texts from this era, such as "Sir Gawain and the Green Knight" and "Piers Plowman," illustrating their contributions to literature through heroic adventures and complex allegories. The chapter then shifts to the emergence of Renaissance humanism, shedding light on the pivotal role of key figures like Dante Alighieri and Geoffrey Chaucer. These figures, through their works, effectively bridged the gap between medieval and Renaissance thought. This exploration allows readers to understand how the Renaissance ushered in a new literary era that emphasised individualism, classical antiquity, and secular themes, thereby forever transforming the literature landscape.

Chivalric Romances and Allegory

The chivalric romance genre, an integral part of medieval literature, vividly encapsulates the values and societal structures of the period. Originating in the Middle Ages, these narratives centred on the heroic exploits of knights who embodied the cultural ideals of valour, honour, and courtly love. Rooted in the medieval tradition, chivalric romances typically revolved around themes of knightly courage and devotion to a noble lady, intertwining personal quests with moral obligations.

Chivalric romance stories often depicted knights as heroic figures, embarking on perilous adventures to prove their worthiness through acts of bravery and loyalty. These narratives were a testament to the valour and courage of these knights, serving as a source of inspiration and admiration for the readers.

Characters like Sir Gawain from "Sir Gawain and the Green Knight" exemplified the quintessential knight, whose strength, moral integrity, and unwavering adherence to the code of chivalry made him a model for audiences to admire and emulate. The narratives were about physical quests and internal battles where knights faced moral dilemmas, balancing personal desires with societal expectations.

Allegorical elements played a significant role in these tales, serving as vehicles for more profound moral and spiritual lessons. Allegories, such as those found in works like "Piers Plowman," provided readers with complex metaphors that conveyed ethical dilemmas and spiritual struggles pertinent to medieval Christian beliefs. These allegorical narratives utilised symbolic characters and events to personify virtues and vices, making abstract concepts more accessible and compelling to the audience. For instance, the character of Lady Fortune in many medieval texts symbolised the capricious nature of fate, reminding readers of the temporal and changeable nature of earthly pursuits.

Chivalric romances also reinforced the social hierarchy and the medieval society's feudal system. The tales often glorified the feudal relationship between lords and vassals, portraying it as an idealised bond of mutual loyalty and respect. Knights, bound by their oaths of fealty, were depicted as paragons of virtue, upholding the stability and order of the hierarchical social structure. In these narratives, the knight's duty to his lord was mirrored by his service to his lady, reinforcing the intertwined notions of personal honour and social duty.

Although often relegated to supporting roles, women in chivalric romances were pivotal in shaping the narrative structure. They frequently represented ideals of beauty, virtue, and unattainability, serving as the primary motivation for the knight's quest. The concept of courtly love elevated the status of women within these tales, idealising romantic love as a noble pursuit that inspired knights to perform great deeds. This dynamic not only reinforced traditional gender roles but also emphasised the importance of honour and social status within the knightly class. Women, such as Guinevere in the Arthurian legends, epitomised the blend of grace and authority, influencing the actions and fates of their male counterparts.

Moreover, the supernatural elements often found in chivalric romances enhanced the sense of adventure and heightened the stakes of the knight's journey. Magical creatures, enchanted objects, and mystical events catalysed character development and plot progression. While providing excitement and wonder, these fantastical components symbolised the moral and ethical tests knights had to overcome to achieve their quests. Elements like Merlin's enchantments in the Arthurian legends added complexity to the narrative, reflecting the belief in a world of divine and mystical significance.

The influence of chivalric romance extended beyond the medieval period, significantly shaping later literary forms during the Renaissance. The ideals of courtly love and heroic adventure embedded in these medieval tales continued to be explored in Renaissance literature, fostering narratives that delved deeper into individual experience and personal choice against the backdrop of societal expectations. Works like Edmund Spenser's "The Faerie Queene" drew upon the chivalric tradition, weaving allegory and adventure together to reflect Renaissance humanism and emerging modern sensibilities.

Ultimately, chivalric romances served as a mirror to medieval society, reflecting its values, ideals, and hierarchical structures. Through tales of knightly valour and courtly love, these narratives celebrated the virtues of honour and bravery, offering audiences both entertainment and ethical instruction. Chivalric romances perpetuated the cultural norms and aspirations that defined the medieval world by portraying knights as embodiments of the era's highest ideals. Allegorical tales, with their rich symbolic layers, provided moral guidance while reinforcing the spiritual and social mores of the time.

Dante's Divine Comedy

Dante Alighieri's "Divine Comedy" is crucial to understanding the transition from medieval to Renaissance literature. This epic poem, composed early in the 14th century, encapsulates themes and structures that weave together the fabric of medieval cosmology while sowing seeds for Renaissance humanism.

The "Divine Comedy" is divided into three parts: Inferno, Purgatorio, and Paradiso. Each segment represents one of the realms of the Christian afterlife, vividly portraying medieval religious beliefs. The structure of the poem itself—each part containing 33 cantos, plus an introductory canto in Inferno—reflects a deep engagement with the symbolic use of numbers, which was prevalent in medieval thought. For instance, the number three holds significant meaning within the Holy Trinity, echoing the medieval mindset deeply intertwined with Christian doctrines.

One central theme throughout the "Divine Comedy" is the soul's journey towards God, embodying the medieval worldview of life as a pilgrimage fraught with moral and spiritual decisions. However, beyond these traditional elements, Dante introduces personal experiences and ethical dilemmas which resonate more with the humanistic focus of the Renaissance. His exile from Florence due to political strife mirrors the turbulent political landscape of 13th-century Italy. It allows him to comment on the nature of power, justice, and corruption through the characters he encounters in Hell, Purgatory, and Heaven. This reflects his belief in the importance of civic responsibility and personal virtue.

Dante's story is an allegory for the individual's quest for meaning and redemption, a precursor to the Renaissance emphasis on personal experience and individualism. His journey, guided by Virgil and later Beatrice, underscores the potential for personal growth through reason and love—a profound departure from purely dogmatic religious teaching.

Dante's choice of guides highlights his blending of classical and Christian traditions. The Roman poet Virgil represents classical wisdom and rationality, reflecting Renaissance admiration for ancient texts and philosophy. This respect for classical antiquity, juxtaposed with Christian theology, signifies a cultural shift. It suggests a synthesis of both traditions that would become a hallmark of Renaissance humanism. By integrating figures from Greek and Roman mythology into his Christian narrative, Dante pays homage to the past and elevates contemporary themes to a level of timeless relevance. This approach bridges the gap between the medieval and the modern, making ancient wisdom accessible and relatable to his readers.

Moreover, Dante's work references classical authors such as Homer, Ovid, and Aristotle. These allusions enhance and imbue the narrative with a sense of universality and continuity. In Canto V of Inferno, for example, Dante's encounter with Francesca da Rimini poignantly explores the potent force of romantic love and its tragic consequences. Here, Dante humanises and dignifies individuals based on their virtues and failings rather than solely on doctrinal judgments. This nuanced portrayal of human nature aligns with Renaissance ideals, emphasising reason, individual dignity, and the complex interplay of human emotions.

One cannot ignore the language in which "Divine Comedy" is written. Dante's decision to write in the vernacular Tuscan dialect instead of Latin democratised literature paving the way for future Italian writers and poets. This act of linguistic defiance contributed significantly to developing a national literary identity for Italy. It demonstrated that great literary works did not need to conform to the exclusivity of Latin, thereby making literature more accessible to the common people. This move also set a precedent for Renaissance writers who sought to address a broader audience.

In addition, Dante's theological insights and advocacy for the separation of church and state influenced the secular tone of Renaissance humanism. Dante anticipated later Renaissance thinkers like Machiavelli, who argued for a pragmatic and secular approach to governance by asserting that temporal and spiritual powers should be distinct. This ideological shift played a crucial role in shaping the intellectual landscape of the Renaissance, promoting a more secular worldview that valued empirical evidence and rational thought over blind faith.

Dante's incorporation of these themes into a cohesive narrative underscores his dual role as a medieval thinker and a forerunner of Renaissance humanism. He engaged with contemporary issues through a lens that combined religious doctrine with personal introspection and classical learning. This sophisticated interplay set the stage for subsequent Renaissance literature, emphasising the value of the individual and the importance of inner virtue.

Geoffrey Chaucer's Canterbury Tales

Geoffrey Chaucer's "Canterbury Tales" is a literary bridge between the medieval and Renaissance periods, encapsulating elements from both eras with remarkable skill. The "Canterbury Tales" structure is one of its most innovative features, using a pilgrimage narrative to bring together a diverse group of characters, each representing different facets of society. This framing device creates a coherent progression through the collection of stories and reflects the societal diversity of Chaucer's time. Pilgrimages were common in medieval Europe, serving both religious and social functions. Chaucer's choice to use this setting allows him to weave together various tales that showcase a cross-section of his contemporary world.

Chaucer employed satire as a powerful tool to critique social norms and hypocrisies prevalent in medieval society. He exposes the flaws and contradictions within various social institutions through his characters' exaggerated traits and behaviours. For instance, the Pardoner, who sells indulgences, embodies the corruption within the Church. His tale and behaviour highlight the gap between the Church's spiritual ideals and the reality of its practices, allowing Chaucer to critique the misuse of religious authority without overtly condemning the institution itself. Similarly, the Knight's portrayal provides a nuanced look at chivalric values, contrasting his noble appearance with behaviours that might appear less honourable upon closer inspection.

Chaucer's use of irony and exaggeration in these portrayals engages readers in a deeper consideration of the true nature of societal roles and norms.

Realism is another hallmark of Chaucer's work, illustrating a growing interest in everyday life and the personal stories of individuals. Unlike many of his contemporaries who focused on lofty ideals and abstract themes, Chaucer delved into the mundane details of his characters' lives. The Miller, for example, is described with vivid physicality, from his stout body to his coarse mannerisms, bringing a sense of authenticity to his character. Chaucer invited his audience to see their world reflected in his tales by creating characters genuinely representative of the people around him. This focus on realism paved the way for later literary works that would further explore individual experiences and personal narratives, aligning with emerging Renaissance humanism that emphasised the value of personal experience and observation.

Chaucer's innovative use of vernacular English was a groundbreaking contribution to literature, making it accessible to a broader audience. Before Chaucer, much of the literature in England was written in Latin or French, languages typically accessible only to the educated elite. By writing in Middle English, Chaucer democratised literature, allowing more people to engage with his stories. This shift had significant implications for developing English literature and establishing English as a legitimate language for scholarly and artistic expression. It also influenced the standardisation of English spelling and grammar, contributing to the linguistic foundation upon which future generations of writers would build. Chaucer's commitment to using the vernacular not only broadened his readership but also helped to shape the cultural identity of England.

The "Canterbury Tales" is a tapestry of tales, reflecting different perspectives and experiences yet connected through the overarching pilgrimage narrative. This structure allowed Chaucer to explore various themes and issues, from the sacred to the profane, without losing the collection's coherence. Each character's tale offers insights into their values, desires, and shortcomings, providing a multifaceted view of medieval society. For example, the Wife of Bath's tale and prologue delve into themes of gender roles and marriage, presenting a complex view of female autonomy and agency. Her bold personality and multiple marriages challenge the traditional views of women in medieval society, making her one of the most memorable characters in the collection.

Through his satirical lens, Chaucer also critiques his time's social hierarchy and class dynamics. The interactions among pilgrims from different social backgrounds reveal tensions and power dynamics that underpin medieval society. Characters such as the Merchant and the Reeve represent the rising middle class, whose economic influence grew as they struggled for social recognition. By juxtaposing these characters with those from traditional noble and clerical classes, Chaucer invites readers to reflect on the changing social landscape and the fluidity of social mobility.

Furthermore, Chaucer's use of a frame narrative in the "Canterbury Tales" enhances the storytelling and adds layers of meaning to the text. The frame narrative allows for a meta-commentary on the act of storytelling itself, as pilgrims share their tales within the context of the pilgrimage. This technique draws attention to the constructed nature of narratives and how stories can convey personal and societal truths. It also enables Chaucer to create a dialogue between the tales, as characters respond to and critique each other's stories, adding depth and complexity to the overall narrative.

The Rebirth of Humanism

Humanistic thought experienced a significant resurgence during the Renaissance, profoundly impacting literature and transforming cultural landscapes. To understand this shift, it is essential to explore the origins of humanism, the contributions of critical thinkers like Petrarch and Erasmus, and how these ideas shaped literary themes and perspectives.

Humanism is a philosophical and cultural movement with roots in classical antiquity, emphasising the value of human experience and the study of classical texts. The term "humanism" itself was coined much later, but the principles it represents were evident during the Renaissance. The revival of ancient Greek and Roman literature, art, and philosophy played a crucial role in shaping the intellectual atmosphere of the time. This shift in focus from medieval scholasticism to classical ideals marked a departure from purely religious studies to a broader exploration of what it means to be human.

Central to this movement were figures like Francesco Petrarch, often regarded as the father of humanism. Petrarch's deep appreciation for classical texts and his efforts to rediscover and promote the works of ancient authors laid the groundwork for Renaissance humanism. His writings emphasised individual self-expression and personal virtue, advocating for a return to the values and wisdom of antiquity. Petrarch believed studying classical texts could lead to a more profound understanding of human nature and morality.

Desiderius Erasmus, another pivotal figure, contributed significantly to developing humanist philosophy. Erasmus shared Petrarch's love of language and classical literature but also sought to reconcile these ideals with Christian thought. His works, such as "The Praise of Folly," criticised the complexities and pretences of medieval institutions while promoting a more personal and introspective approach to faith and knowledge (*Humanism - Desiderius Erasmus | Britannica*, n.d.). Erasmus believed in the importance of education and the power of literature to inspire moral and intellectual growth.

One of the most notable impacts of humanism on Renaissance literature was the increased focus on themes of identity, morality, and the human condition. Writers and poets began exploring the complexities of human emotions and experiences, moving away from the allegorical and didactic narratives in medieval literature. This shift allowed for a more nuanced and realistic portrayal of characters and their struggles, reflecting the humanist belief in the individual's capacity for reason and self-determination.

For example, we see a blend of medieval and emerging Renaissance sensibilities in Geoffrey Chaucer's works. Though rooted in medieval traditions, "The Canterbury

Tales" employs satire and realism to critique social norms and present a diverse array of human experiences. This blending of old and new reflects the transitional nature of the period and the growing interest in individual stories and personal perspectives.

Exploring human emotion and experience during the Renaissance promoted a more secular worldview. While religion remained important, humanists emphasised the value of earthly life and the pursuit of knowledge for its own sake. This secular approach is evident in writers like Michel de Montaigne, whose essays delve into personal reflections and scepticism, questioning established doctrines and exploring the nature of humanity.

Moreover, the humanist emphasis on education and the study of classical texts influenced the literary styles and techniques of the time. The eloquent use of Latin, the practice of philology, and the appreciation for rhetorical skills became hallmarks of Renaissance literature. Writers sought to emulate the clarity and beauty of classical prose while infusing their works with contemporary relevance.

Shakespearean Drama and Poetry

Shakespeare's works stand as quintessential examples of Renaissance literature and thought. His dynamic characters and complex plots offer profound explorations of human experiences. In plays like "Hamlet," "Othello," and "Macbeth," Shakespeare delves into the depths of human emotion and psychology, presenting characters with rich interior lives that reflect the multifaceted nature of humanity. Through Hamlet's existential musings, Othello's tragic jealousy, and Macbeth's ambition-fueled downfall, Shakespeare investigates what it means to be human, portraying individuals who grapple with reason, morality, and fate.

Themes of love, power, and identity recurrently appear in Shakespeare's works, providing a window into Renaissance concerns about the human condition. Love, in its various forms—from the passionate romance of "Romeo and Juliet" to the complex friendship in "The Merchant of Venice"—is a central theme, revealing the era's preoccupation with the idealisation and the complications of human relationships. Power is another prominent theme, explored through narratives of political intrigue and personal ambition, such as in "Julius Caesar" and "Henry V." These stories highlight existential dilemmas, where characters face moral and ethical decisions that resonate across ages. Identity, too, plays a critical role in Shakespeare's oeuvre. Characters often embark on journeys of self-discovery or wrestle with dualities within themselves, as seen in "Twelfth Night" and "The Tempest," where disguise and transformation prompt reflections on selfhood and authenticity.

One of Shakespeare's significant contributions to the Renaissance was his advancement of the English language through inventive vocabulary and idiomatic expressions. He expanded the lexicon by coining new words and phrases, some still in use today. The playful manipulation of language, particularly in his comedies, showcases his linguistic creativity. For instance, terms like "bedazzled," "cold-blooded," and "leapfrog" originated from his inventive mind. Additionally, his works popularised the use of iambic pentameter and blank verse and made substantial strides in standardising spelling and grammar (Maryville University, 2022).

Shakespeare's diverse genres—including tragedy, comedy, and history—have significantly expanded literary boundaries and inspired future generations. His tragedies, such as "King Lear" and "Hamlet," combine romance and tragedy, creating emotionally gripping narratives and layered with philosophical undertones. Comedies like "A Midsummer Night's Dream" and "As You Like It" delve into themes of love and identity with humour and wit, reflecting the lively spirit of the Renaissance. Meanwhile, historical plays like "Richard III" and "Henry IV" dramatise significant events and figures, blending historical fact with creative embellishment to explore leadership, power, and legitimacy themes.

Moreover, Shakespeare's work is deeply influenced by the burgeoning humanist ideas of his time.

Humanism, which emphasises the value of individual experience and expression, is evident in Shakespeare's nuanced portrayals of human nature. Characters in his plays, such as Hamlet, embody the Renaissance belief in the complexity and dignity of the human soul. Hamlet's soliloquies, filled with introspection and philosophical inquiry, showcase the Renaissance preoccupation with individuality and the quest for meaning.

Shakespeare's influence extended beyond his lifetime, shaping the development of modern storytelling and drama. His exploration of universal themes and human experiences has made his works timeless and continuously relevant to contemporary audiences.

Modern adaptations and performances of his plays attest to their enduring impact, demonstrating how Shakespeare's insights into the human condition resonate with new generations. From mainstream films like "West Side Story," which reimagines "Romeo and Juliet," to contemporary retellings in novels and theatre, Shakespeare's legacy continues to inspire and challenge storytellers (Cartwright, 2020).

Summary and Reflections

This chapter has delved into the evolution of literature from the Medieval to the Renaissance period, highlighting critical shifts in themes and narratives. We examined how chivalric romances celebrated knightly heroism and moral integrity, often through allegorical tales that provided ethical guidance. These stories not only reflected but also reinforced the values and social structures of medieval society. The chapter also explored Dante's "Divine Comedy," which merged medieval religious beliefs with the personal introspection characteristic of Renaissance humanism. Dante presented a complex interplay of classical wisdom and Christian doctrine through his journey.

Additionally, we discussed Geoffrey Chaucer's "Canterbury Tales" as a pioneering work that satirically critiqued societal norms while embracing realism and vernacular English. The humanist ideals of the Renaissance brought forth a renewed focus on individual experience and classical antiquity, profoundly influencing literary styles and themes. Shakespeare's contributions further exemplified this shift, using complex characters and inventive language to explore the depths of human emotion and identity. By tracing these transformations, the chapter illustrated how literature evolved to reflect broader cultural and intellectual currents, paving the way for modern storytelling traditions.

Reference List

Chivalric romances - Vocab, Definition, and Must Know Facts | Fiveable. (2024). Fiveable. me. https://library.fiveable.me/key-terms/introduction-to-comparative-literature/chivalric-romances

Chivalric Romance - Vocab, Definition, and Must Know Facts | Fiveable. (2024). Fiveable. me. https://library.fiveable.me/key-terms/medieval-literature/chivalric-romance

Canterbury Tales - Vocab, Definition, and Must Know Facts | Fiveable. (2024). Fiveable. me. https://library.fiveable.me/key-terms/european-art-civilization-after-1400/canterbury-tales

Chaucer and The Canterbury Tales | English 12 Class Notes | Fiveable. (2024). Fiveable. me. https://library.fiveable.me/english-12/unit-2/chaucer-canterbury-tales/study-guide/DqJ6VDuHKU65VKjL

Cartwright, M. (2020, November 4). *Renaissance Humanism* . World History Encyclopedia. https://www.worldhistory.org/Renaissance_Humanism/

How did Dante influence the Renaissance - DailyHistory.org. (n.d.).
Www.dailyhistory.org. https://www.dailyhistory.org/How_did_Dante_influence_the_Renaissance

Maryville University. (2022, May 5). *William Shakespeare's Influence on Contemporary Literature.* Maryville Online; Maryville University. https://online.maryville.edu/blog/william-shakespeare-influence/

Shakespeare and the Renaissance - Engelsk 2 - NDLA. (n.d.). Ndla.no. https://ndla.no/

subject:6e2e2319-cb8a-4dd2-b382-e30f001633bb/
topic:94de9967-1492-479b-b0a8-6764a616b50d/
topic:954b3d73-7652-447c-9fe5-e326ded1ae9a/
resource:61af6f03-cc83-4877-a3bd-a7fc834c5571

Sawyer, N. J. (2010). *Sympathy for the damned: Humanism in Canto V of Inferno.* Retrieved from https://bu.digication.com/nicksawyerdanteportfolio1

humanism - Desiderius Erasmus | Britannica. (n.d.). Www.britannica.com. https://www.britannica.com/topic/humanism/Desiderius-Erasmus

CHAPTER FIVE

THE EVOLUTION OF BRITISH LITERATURE

"The evolution of British literature reveals a rich tapestry of cultural and historical movements that have shaped literary expressions and themes over time. This chapter surveys the key periods and movements within this vast literary landscape, offering insights into how writers have responded to their changing environments. Tracing these developments gives us a deeper understanding of how historical events and societal changes influenced the works produced during each era. By examining these shifts, readers can appreciate the dynamic nature of British literature and its ability to reflect on and critique the world around it."

This chapter delves into several significant periods of British literature, exploring how each contributed to the overall literary heritage. It covers the influential Elizabethan Age, known for its flourishing drama and poetry under the patronage of Queen Elizabeth I. Next, the chapter transitions to the Metaphysical poets of the 17th century, who brought a new intellectual rigour and inventive use of language to poetry. The chapter then moves on to the Restoration and Enlightenment periods, highlighting the rise of satire, the novel, and intellectual inquiry. The Romantic Movement will be explored, emphasising the shift towards emotion, nature, and individualism. Finally, the chapter concludes with the Victorian era, where literature became a powerful social critique and reflection tool. Each section provides a comprehensive overview of the significant works and authors that defined these periods, helping readers understand the evolving nature of British literature.

The Elizabethan Age

The Elizabethan Age remains an iconic period in the history of British literature, known for its groundbreaking literary achievements and profound cultural influence. This era, marked by Queen Elizabeth I's long and stable reign, saw the flourishing of the arts, profoundly impacting English literature through political stability, the birth of iconic playwrights, and the exploration of themes that resonated with societal norms and power dynamics.

Political stability and patronage by Queen Elizabeth I fostered a flourishing arts scene. Her support provided a conducive environment for writers and artists to thrive, free from the constant upheavals that had plagued earlier periods. Elizabeth understood the value of art as a means of personal enjoyment and political propaganda, using it to promote her image and the ideals of her monarchy. This patronage extended to the establishment of theatre companies like The Lord Chamberlain's Men, which later became The King's Men under James I. These companies benefited from royal favour and performed regularly at court, contributing to the elevated status of playwrights and performers alike.

Plays during the Elizabethan Age often mirrored societal issues and offered commentary on governance. The political and social fabric of the time was woven into theatrical productions, providing a platform for discussion and reflection. William Shakespeare's "Julius Caesar" is a prime example. In it, questions about tyranny and democracy are explored, leaving audiences to ponder the nature of power and its consequences.

This spirit of inquiry and debate was fueled by the relative freedom of expression in this era despite specific controversial topics being subject to censorship. Theatre entertained and educated the public, serving as a mirror to contemporary society's complexities and challenges (eNotes, n.d.).

The birth of iconic playwrights like William Shakespeare transformed English literature. Shakespeare's unparalleled genius lies in his ability to elevate the human experience through complex characters and diverse narratives. His works traversed various genres—tragedy, comedy, history—each innovatively tailored to captivate and provoke thought among audiences. For instance, in plays like "Hamlet," existential themes and the human condition are intricately examined, providing timeless reflections on life and death. Alongside Shakespeare, Christopher Marlowe also made significant contributions with his bold, poetic storytelling, best exemplified in

"Doctor Faustus," which delves into themes of ambition and damnation. These playwrights did not merely tell stories; they redefined English literature's narrative structures and linguistic beauty.

Themes of love and power were extensively explored in Elizabethan literature, reflecting societal norms and power dynamics. Love, whether romantic or familial, was a central theme that revealed much about the human psyche and social relations. In Shakespeare's "Romeo and Juliet," the intense passion between the titular characters becomes a poignant commentary on the destructive power of familial feuds and societal expectations. On the other hand, power is dissected in various plays such as "Macbeth" and "King Lear." In "Macbeth," the corrosive nature of unchecked ambition is laid bare. At the same time, "King Lear" examines the devastating effects of power struggles within a family, echoing broader themes of betrayal and authority.

The Elizabethan Age was not just a golden era for drama; it was a period of rich literary diversity and innovation across various forms of writing. Poetry flourished alongside drama, with poets like Edmund Spenser and Philip Sidney creating works that remain cornerstones of English literature. Spenser's "The Faerie Queene" stands out for its allegorical content and intricate verse structure, melding classical influences with contemporary concerns. Sidney's "Astrophel and Stella" set new standards for sonnet sequences, blending personal emotion with philosophical musings.

The influence of historical context on Elizabethan literature must be considered. The religious and political upheavals that defined the preceding Tudor period set the stage for a society eager for stability and expression. The dissolution of the monasteries and the establishment of the Church of England under Henry VIII had far-reaching cultural impacts, influencing themes of authority and faith in subsequent literature. By the time Elizabeth ascended to the throne, these transformations had created a unique cultural landscape ripe for artistic exploration. Literature became a medium through which writers could navigate and comment on the changing world around them.

Furthermore, advancements in printing technology played a crucial role in disseminating literary works. The increased availability of printed materials meant that plays, poems, and prose could reach a wider audience. This democratised access to literature and ensured that the works produced during this period had a lasting impact. Shakespeare's plays, for example, were published in quarto editions and later compiled into the First Folio, preserving them for future generations.

Metaphysical Poets

Metaphysical poetry, a term coined in the 17th century to describe a unique style of poetic expression, is renowned for its intellectual rigour and innovative use of language. This subsection analyses the distinctive characteristics and contributions of the Metaphysical poets, particularly their inventive approach to poetry. The genre's influence on contemporary and later literary movements cannot be overstated.

The Metaphysical poets' wit and intellectual playfulness set them apart from their predecessors and contemporaries. Their verses often engaged readers on a deeper cognitive level, requiring active mental engagement rather than passive consumption. By layering meaning and utilising elaborate metaphors, these poets challenged their audience to think critically about the themes they were exploring. Their work was intellectually stimulating, blending emotion and reason in ways that were unprecedented at the time. One of the central figures of this movement, John Donne, masterfully combined physical and spiritual elements through his use of conceits. His metaphors, known as conceits, were unconventional and original, merging disparate ideas to create new insights into concepts like love and faith. For instance, in "The Flea," Donne compares a flea bite to the physical union, intertwining bodily imagery with a romantic desire to explore complex emotional landscapes.

Another key figure, George Herbert, contributed significantly to the religious dimension of Metaphysical poetry. His exploration of spiritual themes through innovative structuring and figurative language provided a new depth to religious poetry. Poems like "The Collar" exhibit Herbert's ability to weave personal devotion with broader theological issues, using simple yet profound metaphors from everyday life. Herbert's diction often remained straightforward and colloquial, making his profound ideas accessible to a wider audience. His structured approach to religious poetry contrasted with Donne's more complex conceits, offering a different but complementary perspective within the Metaphysical tradition.

One of the hallmark traits of Metaphysical poetry is the intimate blend of personal experience and abstract thought. This fusion allows readers to connect deeply with the poet's insights, bridging individual reflection and universal themes. Donne's reflections on love, death, and divine connection resonate because of their authenticity and intellectual depth. His poems often begin with dramatic openings that catch the reader's attention, pulling them into a world where philosophical inquiry and emotional intensity coexist.

Andrew Marvell, another prominent Metaphysical poet, further expanded the scope of the genre by incorporating political and social commentary into his verse. Poems like "To His Coy Mistress" juxtapose carpe diem themes with reflective meditations on mortality and time. Marvell's clever use of irony and rhetorical argument mirrors the dialectical method, engaging readers in a dialogue beyond the poem.

The spoken quality of Metaphysical poetry also distinguishes it from other forms. This characteristic, often marked by colloquial diction and conversational tone, makes the poems feel immediate and personal. Donne's works, for example, often read like intimate conversations, drawing readers into a shared space of intellectual and emotional exchange. This approach not only makes the poems accessible but also enhances their impact, as readers feel directly addressed and involved in the unfolding discourse.

Henry Vaughan, influenced by Donne and Herbert, contributed his unique voice to the Metaphysical canon. His deep spiritual introspection and use of nature as a metaphorical landscape added layers of meaning to his poetry. Vaughan's works often reflect a yearning for transcendence and a connection with the divine, themes that resonated deeply during the uncertain times of the English Civil War.

T.S. Eliot, a 20th-century poet and critic, played a crucial role in re-establishing the significance of Metaphysical poets. Eliot recognised their originality and intellectual complexity, arguing for their place in the modernist canon.

His critical essays helped bring renewed attention to poets like Donne and Marvell, highlighting their innovative techniques and thematic depth. Eliot employed many of the Metaphysical poets' methods in his writing, illustrating their enduring influence on literary tradition.

The Metaphysical poets also explored themes of human existence, questioning the nature of reality, free will, and divine intervention. Their poetry often reflected a balance between scepticism and faith, mirroring their time's tumultuous religious and philosophical debates. By engaging with these profound questions, they positioned themselves at the frontier of literary and intellectual thought.

The diverse approaches within Metaphysical poetry demonstrate the flexibility and adaptability of the genre. While united by common themes and techniques, each poet brought their unique perspective and style, enriching the movement. This diversity is a testament to the Metaphysical poets' ability to innovate and challenge the literary status quo.

The Restoration and Enlightenment

The Restoration and Enlightenment periods they have shaped British literature, marking significant transitions in themes and styles. These eras brought profound shifts in how literature was perceived and produced, reflecting broader cultural and intellectual movements.

Restoration Comedy is a prime example of the interplay between social morals and theatre during this time. With the monarchy restored under Charles II in 1660, theatres reopened after being closed by the Puritans, igniting a renaissance in drama. These comedies often drew from aristocratic life and were known for their witty dialogue, sexual explicitness, and complex character interactions. They reflected and critiqued societal norms, primarily through the figure of the rake—a charming yet morally dubious character who pursued women as conquests. This genre highlighted the duplicity and superficiality of high society, emphasising wit, charm, and cleverness over virtue. Playwrights like William Congreve were central to this development. His works, such as "The Way of the World" (1700), redefined comedic narratives to mirror societal values, offering sharp commentary on issues like marriage, inheritance, and social status. Congreve's characters navigated a world dictated by social expectations and personal desires, reflecting the tension between individual freedom and societal constraints.

In addition to comedy, the literature of the Restoration was marked by a growing embrace of scientific ideals. This period coincided with the Scientific Revolution, and literature began to reflect a shift towards inquiry, reason, and scepticism. Influential figures like John Locke, whose "Essay Concerning Human Understanding" (1690) emphasised empirical knowledge and human reason, profoundly impacted literary themes. Writers integrated these ideas into their works, fostering a culture of intellectual exploration and debate. This intellectual environment paved the way for the Enlightenment, which celebrated human reason, progress, and the potential for societal reform. Literature from this era often tackled philosophical questions and championed rational thought, mirroring the broader shift towards secularism and away from traditional religious dogma.

The rise of the novel as a literary form during the Enlightenment marked another significant evolution in

British literature. Authors like Daniel Defoe were pioneers in this genre, contributing to narrative innovation and expanding the scope of storytelling.

Defoe's "Robinson Crusoe" (1719) is considered one of the first English novels. It combines adventure with detailed realism, following the protagonist's survival on a deserted island. This work epitomised the novel's potential to explore complex themes—such as human resilience, colonialism, and the nature of civilisation—through engaging and accessible narratives. The novel's emergence also reflected a growing middle-class readership, eager for stories that resonated with their experiences and aspirations.

Literary works during these periods did not merely entertain; they engaged deeply with contemporary intellectual and social currents. For instance, Jonathan Swift's "Gulliver's Travels" (1726) employed satire to critique human nature, politics, and the folly of human endeavours. Through fantastical journeys to fictional lands, Swift dissected the absurdities and contradictions of his society, effectively using fiction as a vehicle for philosophical discourse.

The Enlightenment also saw the flourishing of poetry that embraced reason and clarity. Alexander Pope's verse exemplified this trend. His "Essay on Criticism" (1711) articulated good literary taste and moral philosophy principles, blending poetic artistry with intellectual rigour. Pope's work underscored the Enlightenment belief in the power of literature to refine manners, impart wisdom, and promote ethical conduct.

Moreover, both periods witnessed a reevaluation of human relationships and societal structures. The Restoration period, with its focus on satirical and often cynical examinations of love, honour, and reputation, set the stage for the Enlightenment's more idealistic and reformist tendencies. Satire became an essential tool for writers to expose hypocrisy and advocate for change. Works like Swift's "A Modest Proposal" (1729) offered biting social commentary, leveraging irony and exaggeration to highlight the plight of the poor and criticise the exploitation by the wealthy.

The Romantic Movement

The Romantic Movement emerged in the late 18th and early 19th centuries as a reaction against the Enlightenment's emphasis on rationalism and scientific progress. Central to the Romantic ethos was the belief that emotion, nature, and individualism offered deeper truths about human experience and existence. This period marked a significant shift in British literature, moving away from the stringent intellectualism of the Enlightenment towards a profound appreciation for the natural world, personal emotions, and the unique individual.

Nature was pivotal in Romantic literature, serving as both muse and metaphor. Poets like William Wordsworth found inspiration and solace in the natural landscape, seeing it as a source of spiritual renewal and philosophical contemplation. Wordsworth's poetry often imbued everyday scenes and elements of nature with deep emotional resonance, illustrating how the natural world could evoke powerful feelings and reflections. In his work, he celebrated the sublime beauty of the natural environment, portraying it as a healing force for the human soul and an antidote to the dehumanising effects of industrialisation.

The Romantics championed Emotion and personal connection as essential aspects of the human experience, contrasting sharply with the Enlightenment's focus on reason and logic. The Romantic poets valued spontaneity and the intensity of feeling, often delving into their inner emotions and experiences in their works. This emphasis on emotion is vividly captured in Samuel Taylor Coleridge's "The Rime of the Ancient Mariner," where the protagonist's emotional journey through guilt, redemption, and awe underscores the narrative. Coleridge's exploration of the sublime—an overwhelming sense of grandeur and awe inspired by nature's power—highlights the Romantics' fascination with the vastness and mystery of the natural world.

Another critical aspect of Romantic literature was the depiction of nature's sublimity, reflecting the struggle of individuals within the grand and often overwhelming forces of the natural world. This theme is evident in many of Coleridge's works, where the sublime is a backdrop to human endeavour and introspection. The concept of the sublime, introduced by Edmund Burke, emphasises nature's awe-inspiring might and beauty, which can evoke both fear and admiration. In Coleridge's "Kubla Khan," the depiction of the majestic and mysterious landscape mirrors the poet's inner tumult and creative process, illustrating the Romantic belief in the interconnection between internal emotion and external nature.

Prominent figures such as Lord Byron, Percy Bysshe Shelley, and John Keats further cemented the Romantic ideals through their contributions to literature. Their works collectively underscored the movement's themes of individualism, emotive expression, and the celebration of nature. With his brooding and passionate characters, Byron epitomised the Romantic hero who defied societal norms to pursue personal freedom and self-expression. His narrative poem "Childe Harold's Pilgrimage" explores themes of exile, longing, and the quest for meaning, reflecting the Romantic preoccupation with the individual's struggle against the constraints of society.

Shelley's poetry often grappled with themes of political idealism and visionary change, advocating for personal and social liberation. His works, such as "Ode to the West Wind," emphasise the transformative power of nature and the poet's role as a prophet of change.

Shelley's vivid imagery and impassioned language exemplify the Romantic conviction that poetry could inspire and lead societal evolution.

Keats, whose brief but prolific career left an indelible mark on Romantic literature, is celebrated for his rich, sensual imagery and meditations on beauty and transience. In poems like "Ode to a Nightingale" and "Ode on a Grecian Urn," Keats contemplates the fleeting nature of life and the timeless beauty of art. His work captures the quintessential Romantic tension between the temporal and the eternal, illustrating how personal reflection can transcend individual experience.

Victorian Literature

Literature underwent considerable transformation during the Victorian era, influenced by cultural and historical contexts. This subpoint assesses the period's literature, mainly focusing on how authors engaged with the themes of innovation, moral discourse, and social change.

Authors like Charles Dickens were pivotal in using narratives to highlight social injustices and hardships.

Dickens' novels often depicted the grim realities faced by the poor and marginalised. "Oliver Twist" is a prime example of Dickens portraying the brutal treatment of orphans in workhouses and the criminal underworld they often fell into. Through his vivid storytelling, Dickens entertained and brought societal issues to the forefront, compelling readers to confront the inequalities in their society.

The emergence of the social novel was another significant development during this period, advocating for reform through storytelling. These novels focused on societal problems such as poverty, class disparities, and harsh working conditions. Elizabeth Gaskell's "North and South" addressed the industrial divide between the North and South of England while highlighting labour struggles and class tensions. Writers used the social novel to expose systemic flaws and inspire change, pushing readers to think critically about the world around them.

Serialisation democratised literature and expanded access to a broader reading public. Many Victorian novels were initially published in serialised form, appearing chapter-by-chapter in magazines or newspapers. This format made literature more accessible to those who could not afford to buy complete books. It also allowed writers to reach a broad audience and maintain reader engagement over time. Charles Dickens mastered this technique, ending instalments with cliffhangers, keeping readers eagerly awaiting the next issue. Serialisation didn't just broaden readership; it altered how stories were structured and paced, laying the groundwork for modern episodic storytelling.

Character psychological depth became a prevalent feature in Victorian literature, offering rich, complex portrayals that delved into the human psyche. George Eliot, for instance, is renowned for her deep character studies. In Middlemarch, she explores the intricate motivations and inner lives of her characters, presenting a nuanced picture of Victorian society.

Similarly, Thomas Hardy's works often examined individuals' internal struggles against the backdrop of an indifferent universe. In "Tess of the d'Urbervilles," Hardy delves deeply into Tess's emotional and psychological turmoil, portraying her as a tragic figure caught in the web of fate and societal expectations.

These narratives did not merely entertain; they served as mirrors reflecting the day's pressing issues. The Industrial Revolution brought monumental changes; Victorian literature often mirrored these shifts. Themes of industrial discontent were recurrent, echoing the anxieties and transformations of rapid industrialisation. Novels like Elizabeth Gaskell's "Mary Barton" vividly depicted the struggles of the working class, grappling with the harsh realities of factory life and economic hardship. By bringing these stories to light, authors sought to promote empathy and understanding among their readers, urging them to consider the human cost of progress and modernisation.

Faith, doubt, and the spiritual crisis were prominent themes in Victorian literature, reflecting the era's religious and existential questioning. With scientific advancements challenging traditional beliefs, many literary works explored the dichotomy between faith and doubt. George Eliot's "Middlemarch", for example, juxtaposes religious conviction with emerging secular ideologies, reflecting the spiritual tumult experienced by many during this period. This exploration highlighted the evolving spiritual landscape and the quest for meaning in an increasingly secular world.

Groundbreaking literary techniques and innovations marked Victorian literature. The serial publication model not only changed the way stories were consumed but also influenced narrative structures.

Authors like Wilkie Collins and Charles Dickens thrived under this format, using suspense and cliffhangers to keep their audience hooked. This period also saw the rise of new genres, including detective fiction. Edgar Allan Poe and Arthur Conan Doyle introduced the archetypal detective, creating complex mysteries that captivated readers and laid the foundation for future crime fiction.

Poetry, too, evolved significantly during the Victorian era. While the Romantic poets emphasised emotion and nature, Victorian poets like Alfred and Lord Tennyson adopted a more introspective approach, reflecting societal changes and personal struggles. Poets grappled with themes of love, mortality, and the complexities of the human condition, leaving a lasting impact on the poetic landscape.

The evolution of the novel form was another critical aspect of this period. Authors like George Eliot and Charlotte Brontë pushed the boundaries of narrative storytelling, incorporating complex characterisations and societal critiques. Their works dealt with themes of social justice, psychological depth, and moral ambiguity, fostering a deeper engagement with storytelling.

The sociopolitical influence of Victorian literature cannot be overstated. Unlike modern perceptions of literature as mere entertainment, Victorian works often served as catalysts for social and political change. Acts of Parliament like the Reform Acts found echoes in fictional narratives, with authors advocating for reforms and spotlighting societal injustices through their storytelling.

The "Woman Question" was a central theme in Victorian literary discourse, addressing gender roles and advocating for women's rights. Novels by female writers like Mary Wollstonecraft and George Eliot scrutinised the societal constraints placed on women, contributing to the growing dialogue on gender equality.

Lastly, Victorian literature frequently reflected the themes of imperialism and colonialism, exploring the global narratives shaped by the British Empire. Writers examined the impacts of empire on both colonised subjects and the British populace, shedding light on the complexities of cultural exchange and colonial rule.

Summary and Reflections

This chapter explored the significant periods and movements within British literature, focusing on how the Elizabethan Age shaped literary expressions through its unique cultural and historical contexts. Queen Elizabeth I's political stability provided fertile ground for the flourishing of arts, leading to the emergence of iconic playwrights like William Shakespeare. His and Christopher Marlowe's works transformed English literature with innovative narratives and complex characterisations. Themes such as love and power were deeply examined in plays and poetry, reflecting the societal norms and dynamics of the time.

We also delved into the profound influence of historical events on Elizabethan literature, such as the religious transformations initiated by the Tudor monarchy. Additionally, advancements in printing technology allowed a wider dissemination of literary works, ensuring their lasting impact. This period was not just about drama but also the rise of diverse literary forms, with poets like Edmund Spenser and Philip Sidney making enduring contributions. Thus, The Elizabethan Age is a pivotal era in British literature, marked by its rich creativity and reflection of contemporary cultural landscapes.

Reference List

Bertrand, B. (2024, January 12). *Selecting Prominent Victorian Era Authors for In-Depth Study.* Blog. https://www.lincolncreativewriters.com/blogs/victorian-era-authors/

Britannica. (2022, November 30). *Romanticism.* Encyclopedia Britannica. https://www.britannica.com/art/Romanticism

John Donne, George Herbert, Henry Vaughan: Religious Metaphysical poetry. (n.d.). Www. literature-Study-Online.com. http://www.literature-study-online.com/essays/religious-metaphysical-poetry.html

Metaphysical Poetry. (2021, March 27). Poem Analysis. https://poemanalysis.com/movement/metaphysical-poetry/

Mwewa, M. (2023, January 19). *The Elizabethan World.* Kinnu. https://kinnu.xyz/kinnuverse/culture/shakespeare/the-elizabethan-world/

Restoration and Eighteenth Century English Literature: 1660-1789. (n.d.). Read Great Literature. https://readgreatliterature.com/literature-lists-timelines/restoration-and-eighteenth-century-english-literature-1660-1789/

The Long Eighteenth Century. (n.d.). Eastern Connecticut State University. https://www.easternct.edu/

speichera/understanding-literary-history-all/the-long-eighteenth-century.html

The changing face of the Victorian novel | British Literature II Class Notes | Fiveable. (2024). Fiveable. me. https://library.fiveable.me/british-literature-ii/unit-9/changing-face-victorian/study-guide/JmxjutFDosaVsfeD

eNotes. (n.d.). *How did social and political aspects of the Elizabethan age affect drama?* Retrieved from https://www.enotes.com/topics/elizabethan-drama-fs/questions/what-were-some-of-the-social-and-political-340704

joek16. (2020). *Describe the similarities and differences of the Romantic Movement from the Enlightenment.* Brainly. Retrieved from https://brainly.com/question/14488187

CHAPTER SIX

MODERNISM AND POSTMODERNISM

"Modernism and Postmodernism in literature represent two movements that significantly reshaped literary conventions in response to profound societal transformations. Modernism's innovative approaches emerged from rapid industrialisation and urbanisation when traditional narratives were inadequate for expressing the complexities of the modern world. Writers like Virginia Woolf, James Joyce, and T.S. Eliot turned to new narrative techniques, such as stream of consciousness, to portray the fragmented nature of human experience."

Their works delve into characters' inner lives, emphasising subjective perspectives over objective reality.

In contrast, Postmodernism arose as a reaction to the perceived limitations of Modernist thought and further deconstructed established literary forms. This chapter will explore how postmodern writers used metafiction, unreliable narrators, and pastiche to challenge conventional storytelling. Kurt Vonnegut's "Slaughterhouse-Five" and Thomas Pynchon's "The Crying of Lot 49" exemplify these techniques, inviting readers to question the nature of narrative and the role of the author. By examining the distinctive features and broader cultural implications of both movements, this chapter illuminates how literature evolved to address and reflect the dynamic landscape of the 20th century.

Defining Modernism in Literature

Modernism in literature can be traced back to the late 19th and early 20th centuries, marked by intense changes such as rapid industrialisation and urbanisation. As societies transformed under these forces, modernist writers sought new ways of expressing the complexities of their environment. They turned away from traditional narratives and embraced experimentation and new forms of storytelling that could better capture the fractured reality they perceived.

One of the critical characteristics of Modernism is its emphasis on subjective experience over objective reality. Unlike previous literary movements that prioritised detailed descriptions of the external world, Modernism focused on the inner workings of the human mind. This shift is evident in the frequent use of the stream-of-consciousness narrative style. This technique aims to replicate the flow of thoughts and feelings passing through a character's mind, often unstructured and chaotic. It allows readers to delve deeply into the psychological landscape of characters, providing a more intimate understanding of their experiences and emotions.

The stream-of-consciousness technique was notably employed by significant figures such as Virginia Woolf, whose novels like Mrs Dalloway offer a rich tapestry of thoughts and sensory impressions. James Joyce also made substantial contributions with works like Ulysses, where he masterfully captures the internal monologues of his characters. Although primarily known for his poetry, T.S. Eliot explored similar mental and emotional turmoil themes in works like "The Love Song of J. Alfred Prufrock."

The historical context of Modernism cannot be overlooked. The horrors of World War I and the following disillusionment profoundly impacted writers and thinkers of the time. The war shattered many people's faith in societal norms and values, creating fragmentation and existential questioning. This period of upheaval fueled literary experimentation as authors grappled with their changed realities. Modernist literature often reflects this disillusionment through fragmented narratives and explorations of alienation and despair.

T.S. Eliot's magnum opus, "The Waste Land," is a prime example of how World War I influenced Modernist literature. The poem's structure is deliberately disjointed, mirroring the broken state of post-war society. Eliot's use of obscure allusions and fragmentary images requires readers to engage with the text actively, piecing together meaning from the chaos. This method underscores one of Modernism's central tenets: the reader's role in interpreting and making sense of the work is crucial.

Virginia Woolf's writing similarly reflects the impact of societal changes brought about by industrialisation and war. Her novel "To the Lighthouse" delves into themes of time, memory, and human connection, using introspective prose to convey the characters' inner lives. Woolf's focus on the ephemeral nature of existence and her critique of materialism reveal her deep concern with the spiritual emptiness that she believed characterised modern life.

James Joyce's contribution to Modernism extends beyond his innovative narrative techniques. His portrayal of Dublin in "Ulysses" is a microcosm of contemporary urban life, capturing the mundane and the extraordinary with equal precision. Joyce's intricate wordplay and exploration of language push the boundaries of what literature can achieve, challenging readers to reconsider their relationship with the written word.

These significant figures' collective works highlight Modernism's diverse approaches to exploring subjective experience. While they each bring unique perspectives and stylistic innovations, their shared goal is to depict the complexities of human consciousness in a rapidly changing world. By doing so, they broke away from the constraints of realism and opened up new avenues for artistic expression.

In addition to their contributions, modernist writers were part of a broader cultural movement that included advancements in other art forms. Painters like Édouard Manet and composers like Igor Stravinsky rejected traditional techniques in favour of new modes of expression. This cross-disciplinary experimentation is a hallmark of Modernism, reflecting a widespread desire to find fresh ways of engaging with a transformed world.

The philosophical underpinnings of Modernism are rooted in a reaction against the optimism and rationalism of the 19th century. Influenced by thinkers like Friedrich Nietzsche and Sigmund Freud, modernists questioned established truths and explored the irrational aspects of the human psyche. This philosophical shift is evident in the prevalence of symbolism and ambiguity in modernist literature, which invites multiple interpretations and resists definitive meanings.

Modernism's legacy in literature is profound. It shaped subsequent movements and continues to influence contemporary writing. Its emphasis on individual perception and formal innovation paved the way for later developments such as Postmodernism, which further deconstructed traditional narrative structures and themes. The experimental spirit of Modernism remains a vital force in literature, encouraging ongoing exploration of the human experience through the written word.

Stream of Consciousness Technique

Stream of Consciousness: A Hallmark of Modernist Literature

Modernist literature brought forth a radical shift in narrative techniques, prominently featuring the stream-of-consciousness style. This technique aims to depict human thought processes in their raw, unfiltered form, breaking away from traditional linear narratives. By revealing inner thoughts directly, the stream of consciousness provides readers with an intimate glimpse into characters' minds, portraying their emotions, memories, and associations.

The primary purpose of the stream-of-consciousness technique is to capture the fluidity and chaos of human thought. Unlike structured sentences, our thoughts often come in waves, one idea leading to another through free association rather than a logical sequence. This method mirrors how the mind works, making the narrative more authentic and introspective. For instance, as Elizabeth Delf (2019) highlighted, we don't think in organised sentences like "I am walking to the library." Instead, our thoughts might resemble "cold/bright / walk faster / late again," underscoring the non-linear nature of mental processes.

James Joyce's 'Ulysses' is frequently cited as a quintessential example of a stream of consciousness. Joyce delves deep into the minds of his characters, most notably Leopold Bloom, allowing readers to experience his thoughts as they arise spontaneously. In 'Ulysses,' Joyce masterfully blends sensory perceptions, memories, and reflections, creating a multifaceted portrait of Bloom's psyche. This approach enhances character depth and immerses readers in the character's subjective reality.

Virginia Woolf's 'Mrs. Dalloway' is another seminal work employing this technique. Woolf uses a stream of consciousness to explore her characters' internal lives over a single day. Through Clarissa Dalloway's musings, readers encounter her shifting thoughts about life, death, love, and societal expectations. As noted in a passage from 'Mrs. Dalloway,' Clarissa reflects on her connection to Westminster, seamlessly moving from the sound of Big Ben to recollections of past illnesses (Delf, 2019). This associative thinking enriches the narrative, highlighting Clarissa's complex emotional landscape.

Authors like Joyce and Woolf challenge traditional perceptions of time within narrative structures by employing a stream of consciousness. In conventional storytelling, events unfold in a linear progression.

However, the stream of consciousness allows for a more flexible time treatment. Characters may flit between present experiences and memories, blurring temporal boundaries. This fluidity alters pacing and structure, inviting readers to piece together the narrative puzzle in 'Mrs. Dalloway,' Woolf shifts seamlessly between Clarissa's immediate observations and her reminiscences, creating a tapestry of interconnected moments that reflect the true nature of human consciousness.

The impact of a stream of consciousness on reader engagement is profound. This technique demands active participation by immersing readers in characters' chaotic yet vivid inner worlds. Readers must interpret fragmented thoughts, piece together disjointed memories, and navigate the ebb and flow of emotions. This interactive reading experience fosters a deeper connection between the reader and the characters, miming the intimate act of understanding someone's reflections.

In 'Beloved' by Toni Morrison, the stream of consciousness underscores the psychological trauma and fragmented identity of the character Beloved. Her disjointed and repetitive thoughts, such as "I am not dead / I am not" (Stream of Consciousness—Definition and Examples | LitCharts, 2017), convey her struggle to define her existence. The lack of punctuation in her monologue adds to the sense of urgency and confusion, drawing readers into her tumultuous mental state.

The stream-of-consciousness technique also encourages readers to engage with the text more analytically. As they navigate the intricacies of characters' thoughts, readers are compelled to draw connections and infer meanings beyond what is explicitly stated. This active involvement can lead to varied interpretations, enrich discussions, and enhance critical thinking skills.

Moreover, stream-of-consciousness narrations often incorporate multiple layers of meaning through symbolic imagery and sensory details. For instance, in Ulysses, Joyce uses recurring motifs like water and music to link disparate thoughts and evoke emotional resonance. These elements add depth to the narrative, encouraging readers to delve beneath the surface and uncover underlying themes.

Stream of consciousness remains influential in contemporary literature, as seen in works like Irvine Welsh's Trainspotting and Jonathan Safran Foer's Extremely Loud & Incredibly Close. These modern examples continue pushing traditional storytelling's boundaries, demonstrating the technique's enduring relevance and versatility.

Postmodern Narrative Strategies

Postmodern literature is renowned for its innovative narrative techniques that challenge traditional storytelling methods. Metafiction is a crucial feature of postmodern texts, where the work self-consciously examines its construction. This technique blurs the lines between fiction and reality, inviting readers to question the nature of narrative and the role of the author. Another hallmark is unreliable narrators, who present a skewed or contradictory version of events, compelling readers to piece together the "truth" on their own.

One notable example of metafiction in postmodern literature is Kurt Vonnegut's "Slaughterhouse-Five." The novel intertwines historical events with science fiction elements, presenting an anti-war narrative through the fragmented experiences of its protagonist, Billy Pilgrim. Vonnegut directly addresses his writing process within the text, creating a layered reading experience. Similarly, Thomas Pynchon's "The Crying of Lot 49" employs an unreliable narrator, Oedipa Maas, as she unravels a convoluted conspiracy. The ambiguity and elusive nature of the plot challenge readers to navigate the complex web of characters and events, ultimately questioning the very act of interpretation.

Pastiche and parody are additional tools postmodern authors use to subvert traditional narratives. Pastiche combines various genres, styles, and cultural references, creating a collage-like effect that celebrates and critiques the sources it draws from. On the other hand, Parody imitates established forms and conventions to highlight their absurdities and limitations. Both techniques serve as cultural commentary, reflecting the fragmented nature of contemporary society.

In "Slaughterhouse-Five," Vonnegut employs pastiche by blending historical fiction, science fiction, and autobiography elements. This mixture emphasises the chaotic nature of war and invites readers to engage with the novel on multiple levels. Pynchon's "The Crying of Lot 49" utilises parody to critique modern communication systems and societal structures. The novella's labyrinthine plot and eccentric characters underscore the paranoia and confusion inherent in the search for meaning in a postmodern world.

The strategies employed by postmodern authors encourage readers to interrogate the nature of the text and bring their subjective experiences to interpretation. By eschewing linear narratives and embracing ambiguity, these works demand active participation from readers, who must navigate the intricate layers of meaning and form their interpretations.

Metafiction, for instance, often disrupts the reader's immersion in the story by drawing attention to the artificiality of the narrative. This self-reflexive approach can create a sense of detachment, prompting readers to critically examine the relationship between fiction and reality. In "Slaughterhouse-Five," Vonnegut's insertion of himself into the narrative, along with his commentary on the writing process, forces readers to confront the constructed nature of the story. This technique challenges the conventional notion of the author as an omniscient creator, instead presenting the creation of the text as an ongoing, collaborative process between author and reader.

Unreliable narrators further complicate the reader's task by presenting conflicting or incomplete versions of events. This narrative device undermines the expectation of a coherent, authoritative account, instead highlighting the subjectivity and fallibility of human perception. In "The Crying of Lot 49," Oedipa Maas's fragmented and ambiguous narration mirrors her disorientation and paranoia, compelling readers to sift through the story's layers and discern their interpretations. This approach underscores the postmodern distrust of absolute truths and universal narratives, emphasising the multiplicity of perspectives and meanings.

Pastiche and parody also play crucial roles in engaging readers' critical faculties. These techniques invite readers to recognise the intertextual connections and underlying critiques embedded within the text by juxtaposing disparate elements and mimicking established forms. The playful and subversive nature of pastiche and parody aligns with the postmodern ethos of questioning authority and challenging dominant cultural narratives.

In "Slaughterhouse-Five," the pastiche of genres and styles reflects the fragmented and multifaceted nature of wartime experiences. This blend of elements encourages readers to consider the complexities and contradictions inherent in historical representation. Pynchon's use of parody in "The Crying of Lot 49" serves a similar purpose, exposing the absurdities and limitations of modern societal structures. The exaggerated and humorous portrayal of characters and events invites readers to critically examine the power and control systems that shape their lives.

Furthermore, postmodern literature often incorporates intertextuality, referencing and reworking existing texts to create new meanings and connections. This practice reinforces the idea that all texts are part of a larger cultural conversation shaped by the interplay of influences and interpretations. In "Slaughterhouse-Five," Vonnegut's references to other literary works and historical events situate the novel within a broader cultural context, encouraging readers to draw connections between the text and their knowledge and experiences. Pynchon's allusions to various cultural artefacts and historical figures in "The Crying of Lot 49" similarly invite readers to engage with the text on multiple levels, recognising the interwoven nature of cultural production.

Magical Realism

Magical realism is a fascinating narrative technique that sits at the convergence of reality and fantasy. Its roots are deeply embedded in Latin American literature, and it is characterised by seamlessly weaving magical elements into everyday life, creating an enchanting blend that defies traditional storytelling conventions. This literary mode emerged prominently in the mid-20th century, influenced by historical, cultural, and political contexts unique to Latin America.

The term "magical realism" was first coined in the 1940s by Alejo Carpentier, a Cuban novelist who recognised the distinct fusion of reality and myth in much Latin American writing (The Editors of Encyclopedia Britannica, 2018).

This approach allowed authors to depict a world where the extraordinary coexists matter-of-factly with the ordinary. A classic example can be found in Gabriel García Márquez's seminal work, "One Hundred Years of Solitude." In this novel, Márquez crafts a multi-generational saga where magical events unfold within the mundane setting of the fictional town of Macondo, such as the ascension of Remedios the Beauty to heaven and the continuous insomnia plague affecting the townspeople.

Gabriel García Márquez and Isabel Allende are two of the most significant figures associated with magical realism. Márquez's "One Hundred Years of Solitude" stands out as a cornerstone of this genre, offering readers vivid portrayals of supernatural occurrences treated as everyday life. Similarly, Isabel Allende's "The House of the Spirits" infuses her narrative with magical elements that reflect the rich tapestry of Chilean folklore and history, where ghostly presences and clairvoyant visions intermingle with the political upheavals of the 20th century.

Folklore and tradition play crucial roles in shaping the narratives of magical realist texts. These stories often blur the lines between the real and the fantastic by incorporating myths, legends, and oral traditions. This blending of the ordinary with the extraordinary is seen in Allende's work, where family histories are laced with mystical elements, such as Clara del Valle's prophetic abilities. These cultural motifs enhance the narratives and root them firmly in the indigenous and historical contexts from which they arise. By drawing on local traditions, magical realist writers create a sense of authenticity and depth, allowing readers to experience a simultaneously familiar and otherworldly reality.

Magical realism is a powerful means of cultural expression and critique, particularly in postcolonial contexts. Including magical elements allows writers to question and subvert dominant perceptions of reality imposed by colonial powers. For instance, Márquez's storytelling often critiques social and political injustices in Latin America, delivering a potent commentary on issues like imperialism, corruption, and inequality. Through surreal yet relatable narratives, these authors offer alternative viewpoints that challenge conventional understandings of history and reality.

Furthermore, magical realism enables writers to address the complexities of postcolonial identities and experiences. The dual realities—grounded in the tangible world and the other in the realm of myth and magic—reflect the multifaceted nature of postcolonial societies. For example, Carpentier's "The Kingdom of This World" depicts the Haitian Revolution through the eyes of Ti Noël, an enslaved person, intertwining historical facts with Afro-Caribbean religious beliefs and supernatural occurrences. This narrative strategy highlights the resilience and strength of the conquered and reclaims their stories from the margins of history.

Influence of World Wars on Literature

The impact of the World Wars on literary production, themes, and the evolution of styles in both Modernist and Postmodernist texts is profound and multifaceted. The trauma and disillusionment caused by these cataclysmic events significantly shaped the following literature, influencing writers to explore themes and styles that challenged traditional narratives.

Societal changes brought about by both World Wars and their psychological effects marked a distinct shift in social dynamics. The unprecedented scale of destruction, loss of life, and the psychological burden of warfare left an indelible mark on society. Writers began to reflect these societal shifts in their work, using literature as a medium to process and convey the collective trauma and individual psychological ramifications. The wars shattered illusions of a stable, peaceful world, leading to a pervasive sense of uncertainty and existential dread.

Emergent themes like disillusionment, fragmentation, and the absurd became prevalent in literary works post-World War I and II. Disillusionment with traditional values and institutions was a common sentiment, as the wars exposed the futility and destructiveness of such entities. Fragmentation emerged as a stylistic representation of the fractured human psyche and the disjointed nature of post-war reality. The absurd, reflecting the meaningless and chaotic experiences during and after the wars, found expression in various forms, illustrating the struggle to find meaning in a world irrevocably altered by conflict.

Ernest Hemingway's works are a quintessential example of how literature grappled with loss, trauma, and identity in the aftermath of the wars. In his novel "A Farewell to Arms," Hemingway delves into the romantic yet tragic relationship between an ambulance driver and a nurse against the backdrop of World War I. Hemingway's experiences as an ambulance driver during the war informed his realistic portrayal of the emotional and physical scars inflicted by combat. His terse, understated style conveyed the profound disillusionment and fatalism that permeated the lives of those affected by the war.

War poetry also provides critical insights into the psychological impact of the World Wars. Poets like Wilfred Owen and Siegfried Sassoon used stark, vivid imagery to depict the horrors of trench warfare. Owen's "Anthem for Doomed Youth" portrays soldiers' deaths as brutal and impersonal, likening them to cattle led to slaughter. Sassoon's "Counter-Attack" similarly conveys the gruesome reality of battlefield carnage. These poets sought to counter the glorified, patriotic portrayals of war by revealing its grim and dehumanising aspects.

The reverberations of the wars extended beyond individual experiences to broader societal norms and values. Literature began to question and critique the very foundations upon which pre-war society was built. Virginia Woolf's "Mrs. Dalloway" presents a post-war society grappling with widespread psychological distress, exemplified by the character Septimus Warren Smith, a veteran suffering from severe shell shock or PTSD. Woolf's narrative highlights the disconnect between societal expectations and the internal turmoil experienced by those who lived through the war.

In addition to themes of disillusionment and trauma, the wars prompted a reevaluation of literary styles and techniques. Modernist writers such as T.S. Eliot, whose poem "The Waste Land" encapsulates the desolate, fragmented post-war landscape, employed innovative techniques like stream of consciousness and fragmented narrative structures to mirror the chaos and unpredictability of the contemporary world. Eliot's intricate allusions and dense symbolism underscored modern existence's complexity and fractured nature.

Postmodernist texts, emerging in the latter half of the 20th century, continued to explore themes catalysed by the

World Wars but did so with a sense of irony and scepticism. Postmodernism questioned the ability of language and literature to convey truth or meaning in a fragmented, disillusioned world. Authors like Kurt Vonnegut in "Slaughterhouse-Five" used metafictional techniques and unreliable narrators to blur the lines between reality and fiction, reflecting scepticism towards grand narratives and authoritative discourses.

The literature of the World Wars illustrates the transformative power of conflict on artistic expression. The wars dismantled existing literary conventions and inspired writers to seek new ways to represent the complexities of the human condition. By grappling with themes of disillusionment, trauma, and absurdity, writers provided a nuanced exploration of the war's profound impact on individuals and society. This period of intense literary innovation reflected the tumultuous realities of the times. It paved the way for future explorations of identity, memory, and existential inquiry in both Modernist and Postmodernist frameworks.

Summary and Reflections

This chapter delved into the transformative ideas of Modernism and Postmodernism in literature, highlighting how these movements reshaped traditional narratives and forms. Modernist writers like Virginia Woolf, James Joyce, and T.S. Eliot focused on subjective experiences, often using the stream-of-consciousness technique to give readers a deep insight into the characters' minds. Their works reflected the fragmented realities of their time, driven by societal shifts such as rapid industrialisation and the aftermath of World War I.

Postmodernist authors further deconstructed conventional storytelling methods, employing metafiction, unreliable narrators, and pastiche to challenge readers' perceptions of reality and narrative truth. Figures like Kurt Vonnegut and Thomas Pynchon used these innovative techniques to blur the lines between fiction and reality, encouraging active engagement from readers. Modernism and Postmodernism offered fresh approaches to understanding human consciousness and societal changes, leaving a lasting impact on literary expression.

Reference List

Delf, L. (2019, November 22). *What is Stream of Consciousness? || Oregon State Guide to Literary Terms*. College of Liberal Arts; Oregon State University. https://liberalarts.oregonstate.edu/wlf/what-stream-consciousness

Jaariq. (2023). *What effect did both world wars have on the following literature? Explain, using evidence from the text to support your inferences.* Retrieved from https://brainly.com/question/28581610

J., A. (2023, January 23). *Modernism in Literature.* Essaypro.com. https://essaypro.com/blog/modernism-in-literature

Kuiper, K. (2019, January 17). *Modernism.* Encyclopædia Britannica. https://www.britannica.com/art/Modernism-art

Magic Realism | Encyclopedia.com. (n.d.). Www.encyclopedia.com. https://www.encyclopedia.com/literature-and-arts/literature-other-modern-languages/latin-american-literature/magic-realism

Onion, A. (2018, April 26). *How World War I Changed Literature*. HISTORY. https://www.history.com/news/how-world-war-i-changed-literature

Postmodern literature | Art and Literature Class Notes | Fiveable. (2024). Fiveable. me. https://library.fiveable.me/art-and-literature/unit-5/postmodern-literature/study-guide/y4tvjvMhTIvF4Dp9

Postmodern literature - The Art and Popular Culture Encyclopedia. (2022). Artandpopularculture.com. https://www.artandpopularculture.com/Postmodern_literature

Stream of Consciousness - Definition and Examples | LitCharts. (2017). LitCharts. https://www.litcharts.com/literary-devices-and-terms/stream-of-consciousness

The Editors of Encyclopedia Britannica. (2018, August 17). *magic realism | Definition, Authors, & Facts*. Encyclopædia Britannica. https://www.britannica.com/art/magic-realism

CHAPTER SEVEN

CONTEMPORARY LITERATURE

"Contemporary literature is a profound mirror reflecting the diverse identities and multicultural experiences that define today's global society. Contemporary authors harness their narratives to explore complex themes of identity, representation, and social change in an era marked by cultural convergence and technological evolution. These literary works capture various voices, shedding light on individual and collective experiences across different cultures. By delving into minority perspectives, these stories foster a deeper understanding and empathy among readers, revealing the nuanced realities of marginalised communities."

This chapter examines in depth how cultural, technological, and social changes influence modern literature. It starts by discussing the representation of minority voices in contemporary texts and moves on to how intersectionality shapes characters' experiences. The chapter also highlights innovative narrative techniques that reflect the cultural backgrounds of both authors and characters.

Furthermore, this chapter addresses how contemporary literature responds to societal issues and serves as a form of activism. The narrative concludes by exploring the educational value of diverse literary works and their role in fostering cultural competence and inclusivity among readers and students alike.

Identities and Multiculturalism

Contemporary literature profoundly mirrors the diverse identities and multicultural experiences that define today's global society. The rich tapestry of voices in contemporary texts resonates with readers from various backgrounds, fostering empathy and understanding across different cultures. This narrative journey begins with an in-depth discussion of how minority voices are represented in modern literary works.

Cultural representation is a cornerstone of multicultural literature, where authors from underrepresented communities bring their unique perspectives to the forefront. These narratives offer insight into the lived experiences of marginalised groups, shedding light on issues often overlooked by mainstream literature. For instance, books like "The Hate U Give" by Angie Thomas highlight the struggles of African American youth against systemic racism. Such works not only provide visibility to minority communities but also challenge readers to confront their own biases and preconceptions. By presenting authentic and nuanced portrayals of cultural identities, contemporary literature allows readers to engage with stories that might otherwise remain unheard.

Intersectionality, another crucial element, explores how multiple social identities intersect and influence individuals' experiences. This concept, introduced by Kimberlé Crenshaw, is essential for understanding the complexity of characters in contemporary literature. Authors like Chimamanda Ngozi Adichie weave narratives encompassing race, gender, and class, illustrating how these intersecting identities shape one's reality. In her novel "Americanah," Adichie delves into the life of a Nigerian immigrant in America, highlighting the dual challenges of navigating racial and gendered spaces. Stories like these underscore the importance of recognising intersectionality in literature, as they provide a more comprehensive view of the human experience, revealing how different forms of oppression overlap.

The identities of characters and authors significantly influence contemporary literature narrative techniques. Storytelling's style and structure often reflect the creators' cultural backgrounds and personal experiences. For example, the nonlinear narrative in Tommy Orange's "There There" mirrors the fragmented history and dislocated identity of Native Americans. Similarly, magical realism in Latinx literature stems from cultural storytelling traditions that blend the mystical with the mundane, as seen in Gabriel Garcia Marquez's works. These innovative narrative approaches enrich the reading experience, making it immersive and thought-provoking. They challenge traditional storytelling norms, pushing readers to explore new dimensions of narrative art.

Literature also serves as a robust response to societal changes. Contemporary works often address current social issues, offering critiques and commentary on the world around us. They act as a form of activism, raising awareness about injustices and inspiring movements for change. For example, feminist literature has evolved to include diverse voices advocating gender equality across different cultures and contexts. Works like Roxane Gay's "Bad Feminist" critique societal norms while advocating for more inclusive definitions of feminism. Furthermore, dystopian novels such as Margaret Atwood's "The Handmaid's Tale" warn of the dangers of authoritarianism and patriarchy, resonating deeply in today's socio-political climate.

Through these narratives, literature reflects and shapes public discourse, encouraging readers to question and transform the status quo.

Contemporary literature's impact extends beyond mere representation and critique; it fosters cultural competence among readers. By engaging with diverse narratives, readers develop a deeper understanding and appreciation of cultures different from their own. This educational value is particularly significant in academic settings, where multicultural literature can provide students with a broader perspective on global issues. Incorporating these texts into curricula can create more inclusive learning environments that validate all students' identities, promoting empathy and mutual respect.

Moreover, contemporary literature empowers underrepresented authors, allowing them to reclaim their narratives and assert their identities. This empowerment is evident in the increasing popularity of memoirs and autobiographies by authors from marginalised communities. Books like "Becoming" by Michelle Obama and "I Am Malala" by Malala Yousafzai offer personal insights into the lives of iconic figures, inspiring readers with their resilience and courage.

These works highlight the importance of self-representation in literature, demonstrating how personal stories can inspire and mobilise collective action.

Representation plays a vital role in shaping young minds in children's literature. Diverse books enable children to see themselves reflected in the stories they read, fostering a sense of belonging and self-worth. Initiatives like We Need Diverse Books to advocate for greater inclusion in children's publishing, ensuring that all kids have access to stories that resonate with their experiences. Books like "Last Stop on Market Street" by Matt de la Peña and Christian Robinson show the beauty of everyday diversity through engaging and relatable narratives. Such efforts underscore the transformative power of literature in nurturing the next generation's understanding of equity and inclusion.

The translation and dissemination of works across different languages and cultures facilitate the global reach of contemporary literature. Translated literature bridges cultural divides, allowing readers to access many stories worldwide.

Authors like Haruki Murakami and Elena Ferrante have gained international acclaim, bringing Japanese and Italian cultural narratives to a broad audience. This cross-cultural exchange enriches the literary landscape, broadening readers' horizons and fostering a global scholarly community.

Narrative Innovation

Contemporary literature is marked by a surge of innovative narrative techniques and structures pushing traditional storytelling's boundaries. Authors are constantly exploring new ways to captivate readers, creating works that reflect the dynamic nature of modern society. One significant trend in contemporary literature is the adoption of experimental narratives.

These narratives often defy conventional plot structures and character developments, opting for fragmented, non-linear, or disjointed storylines.

Experimental narratives challenge readers to engage with the text in ways that traditional narratives do not. For example, novels like Italo Calvino's "If on a Winter's Night a Traveler" immerse readers in many beginnings without reaching a singular ending. This type of narrative invites readers to piece together the story from scattered fragments, creating a more interactive and participatory reading experience.

Similarly, writers such as David Mitchell in "Cloud Atlas" employ nested stories within stories, each layer adding depth and complexity to the overarching narrative. This approach can make the reading experience more challenging and rewarding, as it requires active engagement and critical thinking.

Another notable technique in contemporary literature is the use of multiple perspectives. By presenting diverse viewpoints within a single narrative, authors can offer more prosperous and nuanced insights into their characters and themes. This technique allows readers to understand the story from various angles, enhancing their empathy and comprehension. In novels like "As I Lay Dying" by William Faulkner, the same events are recounted through the eyes of different characters, each bringing their unique perspective and voice to the narrative. This multiplicity of viewpoints deepens character development and reflects the complexities of real-life experiences, where truth is often subjective and multifaceted.

The integration of technology has also significantly influenced contemporary narrative forms. Digital tools enable authors to experiment with multimedia elements, combining text with images, videos, hyperlinks, and interactive components. This convergence of digital media and literature has given rise to what is known as networked narratives. These narratives span multiple platforms and devices, creating an interconnected web of content that readers can explore non-linearly. A prominent example of this is Mark Z. Danielewski's "House of Leaves," which incorporates an array of footnotes, appendices, and visual texts, mimicking the fragmented nature of digital media and encouraging nonlinear reading practices (Özbilen, 2024).

Additionally, social media has become a fertile ground for literary innovation. Authors are creating fictional social media pages for their characters, allowing readers to interact with them in real time and extending the narrative beyond the confines of the book. This transmedia storytelling enhances reader engagement and provides a more immersive experience, blurring the lines between fiction and reality. Furthermore, democratising publishing through digital platforms like Wattpad and Amazon Kindle Direct Publishing has allowed a more comprehensive range of voices to be heard, including those from marginalised communities. This inclusivity fosters a more dynamic and diverse literary culture where experimentation and innovation can thrive.

Genre blending is another crucial element in contemporary literature, reflecting a growing trend towards hybrid texts that cross conventional genre boundaries. This technique integrates elements from different genres to create something unique and compelling. Genre blending enriches the narrative, challenges readers' expectations, and broadens their understanding of what literature can be. For instance, novels such as "The Road" by Cormac McCarthy combine dystopian fiction and literary prose elements to create a haunting and evocative story. Similarly, Margaret Atwood's "The Blind Assassin" merges historical fiction, romance, and science fiction, resulting in a complex, multi-layered narrative that defies easy categorisation (Greene, 2024).

The appeal of genre blending lies in its limitless creative potential. By drawing from a diverse palette of genre elements, writers can craft original and engaging stories. This approach allows for a dynamic storytelling space where the suspense of a thriller can coexist with the emotional depth of a drama or the imaginative scope of science fiction. Such hybridity reflects the multifaceted nature of human experience, offering readers new and unexpected narrative journeys.

Digital and Interactive Literature

The emergence of digital and interactive literature marks a significant transformation in contemporary reading and writing experiences. This subpoint delves into how technological advancements reshape these experiences, opening new avenues for creativity and reader engagement. By exploring electronic literature (e-literature), interactivity, transmedia storytelling, and the challenges posed by digital formats, we can gain a comprehensive understanding of this dynamic field.

E-literature signifies the evolution of traditional text-based narratives into electronic forms that utilise digital devices for creation, distribution, and consumption. Unlike conventional print literature, e-literature often incorporates multimedia elements such as images, audio, video, and animations, offering a rich, immersive experience. Works like Michael Joyce's "Afternoon, a Story" introduced hypertextual structures, allowing readers to navigate non-linear storylines. Similarly, Shelley Jackson's "Patchwork Girl" reinterpreted classic narratives, demonstrating the versatility of digital literature (Kangune et al., 2023). These examples underscore the unique nature of e-literature, which breaks free from linear constraints and embraces a fluid narrative structure.

Interactivity is a cornerstone of digital literature, transforming passive reading into an engaging participatory experience. Readers are no longer content consumers; they become active participants who shape the narrative's progression through their choices. Interactive features like clicking on links, making decisions, or navigating branching storylines enhance reader engagement and immersion. Digital storytelling platforms often provide tools for authors to craft stories that adapt to reader input, fostering a deeper connection with the text. For instance, hypertext fiction allows readers to explore different narrative paths, creating a personalised reading journey. This shift from passive consumption to active participation highlights the potential of digital literature to engage readers in novel ways (Sanchez-Lopez et al., 2020).

Transmedia storytelling further expands the boundaries of digital literature by spreading narratives across multiple platforms. This approach leverages various media, including books, films, video games, social media, and websites, to create a cohesive story experience. Each medium contributes a unique perspective to the overall narrative, enriching the storytelling process. A prime example is the "Harry Potter" franchise, which extends beyond books into movies, video games, and theme parks, allowing fans to immerse themselves in J.K. Rowling's wizarding world through different lenses. Transmedia storytelling enables authors to reach diverse audiences and offers readers multifaceted ways to engage with the story, making it an integral aspect of modern digital literature.

However, the rise of digital literature has its challenges. One major critique is the issue of accessibility, as not all readers have equal access to digital devices and stable internet connections.

Economic disparities and technological limitations can hinder the widespread adoption of digital literature, potentially excluding specific demographics.

Additionally, there are concerns about the preservation of digital works. Unlike physical books that can last decades, digital formats are vulnerable to technological obsolescence and data corruption. Ensuring the long-term preservation and accessibility of digital literature requires ongoing efforts in archiving and maintaining digital infrastructure.

Moreover, the interactive nature of digital literature raises questions about authorial control and the reader's role. Traditional literary works are typically authored with a clear, linear narrative structure, allowing the author to guide the reader through a predetermined storyline. In contrast, digital literature often relinquishes some degree of control to the reader, who can influence the narrative's direction. This collaborative storytelling approach can lead to fragmented or inconsistent narratives, challenging the conventional notions of authorship. Balancing reader agency with authorial intent is a delicate task that digital literature must navigate.

Despite these critiques, digital literature presents exciting opportunities for innovation in storytelling. Emerging technologies such as artificial intelligence (AI), augmented reality (AR), and virtual reality (VR) are poised to revolutionise the narrative landscape. AI can develop adaptive storylines that respond to reader behaviour, while AR and VR offer immersive environments where readers can interact with characters and settings in unprecedented ways. These technologies promise to create unparalleled narrative experiences that blur the lines between reality and fiction, pushing the boundaries of what literature can achieve.

Experimental Poetry

Contemporary poetry is in a dynamic flux, constantly evolving and challenging traditional forms and conventions. This exploration of current trends in poetry highlights how poets push boundaries and redefine what poetry can be. By examining the manipulation of form, the playful use of language, the reflection of social and political themes, and the influence of digital technology, we can comprehensively understand contemporary poetic expression.

Firstly, contemporary poets are increasingly experimenting with form and structure, breaking from established norms to create innovative and often unconventional works. This manipulation of the form includes playing with line lengths, spacing, and visual presentation on the page, as seen in the works of poets like E.E. Cummings and Marianne Moore. Such experimentation allows poets to create new rhythms and patterns that challenge readers' expectations and encourage them to engage with the text uniquely. For example, some modern poems' fragmented, collage-like structures can evoke a sense of disorientation or complexity, reflecting the multifaceted nature of contemporary life.

Additionally, language play is a prominent feature of contemporary poetry. Poets utilise linguistic creativity to add depth and layers of meaning to their work. This can involve inventing new words, using puns, or exploiting the multiple meanings of words to create rich, textured poems. The avant-garde movement known as Language poetry, which emerged in the late 1960s, exemplifies this approach. Language poets like Lyn Hejinian and Ron Silliman focus on the materiality and musicality of language, using techniques such as parataxis—arranging words and phrases without conventional grammatical connectors—to produce a sense of disjunction and encourage readers to derive meaning from the juxtaposition of fragments. These innovations push readers to think critically about language and its role in shaping our experiences and perceptions.

Social and political themes also play a significant role in contemporary poetry, with many poets using their work as a platform to address pressing societal issues. Experimentation in poetry often mirrors the complexities and conflicts of the modern world, allowing poets to explore topics such as gender inequality, racial injustice, and environmental concerns. For instance, Adrienne Rich's "Diving into the Wreck" uses the metaphor of an underwater journey to confront patriarchal oppression and advocate for female empowerment. Similarly, Audre

Lorde's "Coal" combines her identities as a Black woman and lesbian to speak against both racism and sexism. These poems not only highlight the personal struggles of individuals but also resonate with broader social movements, underscoring the potential of poetry to inspire change and raise awareness about critical issues.

Furthermore, the advent of digital technology has profoundly impacted poetic practices, giving rise to new forms and modes of dissemination. In the "postprint era," digital and social media platforms have expanded the reach of poetry, enabling poets to connect with audiences in innovative ways. This shift is exemplified by the success of InstaPoetry, where poets like Rupi Kaur share their work on Instagram, reaching millions of readers globally. Kaur's debut collection "Milk and Honey" initially gained popularity online before becoming a bestseller, demonstrating how the internet has democratised the distribution of poetry and fostered diverse voices within the global community. Another example is Warsan Shire, whose evocative poems on themes of migration and identity found an audience on Tumblr before being featured in Beyoncé's visual album "Lemonade." These cases illustrate how digital platforms can amplify marginalised voices and provide new opportunities for poetic expression.

The influence of technology extends beyond distribution, also affecting the creation and presentation of poetry. Digital tools allow for multimodal and intermedial forms of poetry, blending text with images, sound, and other media. This broadening of the genre can be understood as a response to the digitalisation of culture, calling for aesthetic experiences that deviate from traditional script and book culture. Poets like Nora

Gomringer, who began in poetry slam and now produces spoken-word poetry disseminated through CDs, the internet, and live events, exemplify this trend. The coexistence of conventional and media-oriented poetry reflects the pluralistic nature of contemporary literary practice and underscores the adaptability of poets in navigating different formats.

Globalisation and Literature

The era of globalisation has had a profound impact on literature, driving an unprecedented level of cultural exchange and interconnectedness. This subpoint analyses the effects of globalisation on contemporary literary works, exploring how global connections inform and transform these works.

Cross-cultural influences in literature are evident as authors from different parts of the world draw upon diverse cultural elements to create unique narratives. Literature today often transcends geographical boundaries, weaving together themes, settings, and characters that reflect a mélange of cultures. For instance, authors such as Chimamanda Ngozi Adichie and Haruki Murakami incorporate elements from their respective Nigerian and Japanese backgrounds while engaging with broader, universal experiences. Such cross-cultural narratives enrich the literary landscape and foster a deeper understanding of various cultural perspectives among readers. The fusion of cultural motifs and storytelling techniques creates a rich tapestry of global literature that epitomises the essence of contemporary writing.

Themes of displacement and belonging are prevalent in contemporary literature, often reflecting the complex realities of a globalised world. Writers grapple with issues of identity, migration, and home, portraying characters who navigate the challenges of living between multiple cultures. The experience of displacement, whether voluntary or forced, significantly influences narratives of identity. For example, Khaled Hosseini's "The Kite Runner" delves into the struggles of Afghan refugees, highlighting the sense of loss and the quest for belonging in a foreign land. Similarly, Jhumpa Lahiri's works frequently explore the cultural dislocation experienced by Indian immigrants in America, offering insights into their efforts to reconcile their heritage with their adopted culture. These themes resonate deeply with readers, many of whom may have experienced similar feelings of displacement and searching for a place to belong.

Language and translation play crucial roles in the global literary landscape, facilitating the dissemination of diverse stories across linguistic barriers. Translating literary works into different languages enables a broader audience to access and appreciate narratives worldwide. This practice enriches the global literary market by introducing readers to varied cultural contexts and storytelling traditions. The translation of Gabriel Garcia Marquez's "One Hundred Years of Solitude" into English is a prime example, which helped popularise magical realism and influenced countless writers worldwide (admin, 2024). However, translation also presents challenges, particularly in preserving the nuances and cultural specificities embedded in the original text. Translators must balance fidelity to the source material and make the story accessible to a new audience.

Despite these challenges, translation remains vital in fostering global literary exchanges and expanding readers' horizons.

Global globalisation has significantly reshaped The global literary market, impacting how literature is produced, distributed, and consumed. International literary festivals, such as the Jaipur Literature Festival, promote cultural exchange by bringing together writers, publishers, and readers from different countries (Globalization and Contemporary Arts | Art and Literature Class Notes | Fiveable, 2024). These events facilitate dialogue and collaboration, enhancing the visibility of diverse voices in the literary world.

Furthermore, global literary prizes, like the Nobel Prize in Literature, influence reading trends and canon formation, elevating the status of works from various cultural backgrounds. Book fairs, such as the Frankfurt Book Fair, provide platforms for international publishing deals, ensuring that notable works reach a global readership (Globalization and Contemporary Arts

| Art and Literature Class Notes | Fiveable, 2024). Digital literary events and online platforms have further democratised access to literature, allowing readers worldwide to participate in literary discussions and engage with authors directly.

Economic aspects of globalisation also play a significant role in shaping the production and consumption of literature. The global literary market operates across borders, with international economic trends influencing publishing practices and reader preferences. Intellectual property rights and funding models have adapted to the challenges of a globalised world, ensuring that authors receive fair compensation for their work while facilitating the dissemination of literature across different markets. Crowdfunding platforms and corporate sponsorships have emerged as new sources of funding for literary projects, enabling writers to reach a broader audience and secure financial support for their endeavours. These shifts in funding and patronage reflect the changing dynamics of the global literary market, driven by the increasing interconnectedness of our world (Globalization and Contemporary Arts | Art and Literature Class Notes | Fiveable, 2024).

Summary and Reflections

This chapter has delved into contemporary literature's dynamic themes and developments, highlighting the profound impact of cultural, technological, and social changes. By examining how minority voices are represented, the role of intersectionality, and innovative narrative techniques, readers understand how modern literature reflects diverse identities and multicultural experiences. The discussion underscores the importance of authentic portrayals and literature's decisive role in fostering empathy and challenging societal norms.

Moreover, contemporary literature's response to societal changes, through works addressing current social issues, demonstrates its function as both a mirror and a catalyst for change. Including underrepresented authors and the global reach of translated works further enrich the literary landscape, promoting inclusivity and global awareness. As students, educators, and lifelong learners engage with these texts, they are encouraged to explore new dimensions of narrative art and develop a nuanced appreciation for the diverse stories that shape our world.

Reference List

Altun, M. (2023). *Literature and identity: Examine the role of literature in shaping individual and cultural identities. International Journal of Social Sciences and Educational Studies,* 10(3), 381-385. https://doi.org/10.23918/ijsses.v10i3p381

Globalisation and contemporary arts | Art and Literature Class Notes | Fiveable. (2024). Fiveable. me. https://library.fiveable.me/art-and-literature/unit-11/globalization-contemporary-arts/study-guide/VQd1UmA5QCIydOnm

Greene, W. (2024, April 30). *A Tale of Two Genres: Mastering the Art of Mixing and Matching in Writing.* Medium; Medium. https://medium.com/@wilbur.greene/a-tale-of-two-genres-mastering-the-art-of-mixing-and-matching-in-writing-a2af3de10bd9

Mwewa, M. (2023, June 28). *Contemporary Poetry.* Kinnu. https://kinnu.xyz/kinnuverse/culture/poetry-a-beginners-guide/contemporary-poetry/

Multicultural literature - Vocab, Definition, and Must Know Facts | Fiveable. (2024). Fiveable. me. https://library.fiveable.me/key-terms/race-ethnicity-politics-in-african-diaspora/multicultural-literature

Poetry in the digital age. (2021, May 21). INSL. https://lyricology.org/poetry-in-the-digital-age/

Salunkhe, P. Y., & Kangune, B. (2023). *Digital literature evolution: Pioneering effective storytelling.* Retrieved from https://www.researchgate.net/publication/377233679_Digital_Literature_Evolution_Pioneering_Effective_Storytelling

Sanchez-Lopez, I., Perez-Rodriguez, A., & Fandos-Igado, M. (2020, September). *The explosion of digital storytelling. Creator's perspective and creative processes on new narrative forms.* Heliyon. https://doi.org/10.1016/j.heliyon.2020.e04809

admin. (2024, June 17). *The Influence of English on World Literature - 5 Minute English . 5 Minute English.* https://5minuteenglish.com/the-influence-of-english-on-world-literature/

Özbilen, D. K. (2024). *Narrative innovations in the digital age: An analysis of the effectiveness of social media on contemporary English fiction. International Journal of Enhanced Research in Educational Development,* 12(4), 2320-8708. https://doi.org/10.55948/IJERED.2024.0709

CHAPTER EIGHT

LITERARY CRITICISM AND THEORY

"Literary criticism and theory provide essential tools for understanding and interpreting texts. This chapter delves into the key concepts and methodologies of various schools of scholarly thought, equipping students with diverse analytical approaches. By examining different perspectives, readers can develop a more nuanced understanding of literature's multifaceted nature."

This chapter starts with Formalism and New Criticism, two text-centred approaches that focus on the intrinsic features of literature, such as form, style, and structure. Students will learn to analyse texts through close readings, paying attention to literary devices and narrative techniques. Key figures within these movements, including John Crowe Ransom and Cleanth Brooks, are discussed to illustrate their influential ideas. The chapter also addresses critical concepts like intentional fallacy and affective fallacy, emphasising the importance of evaluating texts based solely on their content. Through practical applications and classroom exercises, students will gain a deeper appreciation for the craftsmanship involved in literary creation.

Formalism and New Criticism

Formalism and New Criticism: Text-Centered Analysis

Formalism and New Criticism represent pivotal schools of thought in literary theory. They emphasise a text's intrinsic features. They encourage students to explore literature by focusing on form and style independently of historical, biographical, or social context. This approach provides a structured methodology for analysing texts, fostering a deep appreciation for the craftsmanship involved in literary creation.

Definition of Formalism

Formalism is a method of literary criticism that insists on analysing a text based solely on its structure, language, and literary devices. It disregards external context, such as an author's biography or historical background. The primary focus is on how elements within the text work together to create meaning. By examining aspects like symbolism, metaphor, rhyme schemes, and narrative techniques, formalists argue that the essence of a literary work can be understood through its form alone. This approach allows readers to appreciate the text as a self-contained entity with inherent value.

Key Figures in New Criticism

New Criticism developed as an influential movement in the early to mid-20th century, gaining prominence through the work of several notable critics. One of the leading figures was John Crowe Ransom, whose essay "Criticism, Inc." called for a systematic approach to literary analysis free from extrinsic influences. Another seminal contributor was Cleanth Brooks, mainly through his work "The Well Wrought Urn," which explores how form and content are inseparable in poetry. Brooks and Robert Penn Warren co-authored "Understanding Poetry," a critical text cemented New Criticism's place in academic settings. T.S. Eliot's essays also played a crucial role, particularly "Tradition and the Individual Talent," which argued for the objective evaluation of texts. These critics collectively developed principles that have had a lasting impact on literary studies.

Application in Literary Analysis

Applying formalist techniques to literary analysis involves meticulously examining a text's formal elements. For instance, consider William Shakespeare's "Sonnet 18." A formalist reading might explore how the poem's structure—quatrains and final couplet— contributes to its theme of immortalising the beloved through verse. The recurring use of iambic pentameter and the strategic placement of metaphors and similes add layers of meaning within the poem's strict form. The reader can uncover profound insights into the text's artistry by focusing on these elements.

Similarly, applying New Critical methods to F. Scott Fitzgerald's "The Great Gatsby" reveals the novel's intricate narrative techniques and symbolic motifs that speak to themes of aspiration and disillusionment.

Analysing how Fitzgerald uses imagery, such as the green light at Daisy's dock, and motifs like the eyes of Dr. T.J. Eckleburg, allows readers to derive meaning directly from the text itself without relying on external information about Fitzgerald's personal life or the societal context of the 1920s.

In classroom settings, students might be tasked with closely reading specific passages and identifying and interpreting literary devices such as irony, paradox, and allusion. This exercise reinforces the idea that a thorough understanding of form and style can yield rich interpretive rewards. For example, when studying Emily Dickinson's poem "Because I Could not Stop for Death," students might focus on the poem's meter, personification, and use of dashes to understand how these formal choices enhance its meditative exploration of mortality.

Critical Concepts

Two critical concepts central to New Criticism are the intentional and affective fallacy. These ideas advocate for an analytical framework that excludes authorial intent and reader response from consideration.

Intentional Fallacy

Coined by W.K. Wimsatt and Monroe Beardsley, the intentional fallacy refers to the erroneous belief that a critic can accurately determine an author's intended meaning for a text. New Critics assert that a literary work should be evaluated based on the words on the page rather than any presumed intentions of the author. This perspective maintains that meanings conveyed by the text may transcend or even contradict what the author envisages. For instance, while analysing Herman Melville's "Moby Dick," the focus would be on the novel's complex symbolism and stylistic choices rather than Melville's motivations for writing it.

Affective Fallacy

The affective fallacy, also introduced by Wimsatt and Beardsley, describes the mistake of equating a text's value with the emotional responses it elicits from readers. New Critics argue that subjective reactions should not influence the objective analysis of a literary work. Instead, the text's merit lies in its formal qualities and the coherence of its internal structure. In this view, a poem like T.S. Eliot's "The Waste Land" should be studied for its dense allusions, fragmented style, and thematic complexity rather than how it makes individual readers feel.

Structuralism and Semiotics

This section explores Structuralism and Semiotics, critical theories that have profoundly influenced literary criticism. Our goal is to help students understand how meaning is constructed through language and overarching structures.

Basics of Structuralism

Structuralism originated from the linguistic theories of Ferdinand de Saussure, a Swiss linguist whose work laid the foundation for this school of thought. Saussure introduced the concept that language is a system of signs composed of the "signifier" (the form of a word or phrase) and the "signified" (the mental concept it represents). This system operates on the principle that meanings are created through differences within a network of signs, rather than through direct reference to objects or ideas.

Structuralism asserts that all elements of human culture, including literature, can be understood as parts of a larger, underlying structure. By analysing these structures, we can uncover the rules and conventions that govern the creation of meaning. Claude Lévi-Strauss extended these principles to anthropology, examining kinship systems and myths to reveal universal patterns in human societies.

Role of Semiotics

Semiotics, the study of signs and symbols, further elaborates on Saussure's ideas by exploring how meaning is constructed and interpreted. Whereas Structuralism focuses on the relationships between elements within a system, Semiotics delves into the broader context of signification, considering linguistic signs and visual and cultural codes.

Scholars like Roland Barthes significantly developed semiotic theory, which they applied to various forms of media and literature. Barthes' work emphasised how texts communicate through a network of signs, often referencing broader cultural myths and ideologies.

For instance, in his analysis of advertisements, Barthes demonstrated how images and words convey complex messages about societal values and consumer culture (Chandler, 1994).

Semiotics also distinguishes between different types of signs: icons (which resemble what they represent), indexes (which have a causal or existential relationship with their referent), and symbols (which rely on arbitrary connections established by convention).

Understanding these distinctions helps us interpret how texts use signs to create meaning and evoke responses from readers.

Comparative Examples

Let's examine some comparative examples to grasp the practical application of Structuralism and Semiotics. Consider the analysis of a classic text such as Shakespeare's "Hamlet." From a structuralist perspective, one might focus on the play's syntagmatic relations—how scenes and events are organised sequentially—and paradigmatic relations, such as the opposition between characters like Hamlet and Claudius. These relationships reveal the underlying structure of the narrative, highlighting themes of revenge, madness, and power dynamics.

On the other hand, a semiotic analysis would examine the signs and symbols within the text. For instance, the recurring motif of Yorick's skull can be seen as an indexical sign that points to themes of mortality and the inevitability of death. Interpreting these signs within the broader cultural context of Elizabethan attitudes toward death and the afterlife can give us deeper insights into the play's meaning.

Another example is the use of semiotics in visual media, such as film. In Alfred Hitchcock's "Psycho," the infamous shower scene is rich with semiotic significance. The knife, as an index, directly connects to violence and horror, while its rapid movement creates an iconic representation of danger. The stark contrast between light and shadow also enhances the symbolic undertones of good versus evil. By applying semiotic analysis, we can decode the layers of meaning embedded in this iconic scene, understanding how Hitchcock manipulates signs to elicit emotional responses from the audience.

Influence of Cultural Codes

Cultural codes play a crucial role in shaping how we interpret and understand texts. These codes encompass the shared beliefs, values, and norms within a society that influence our reading practices. Structuralism and Semiotics both emphasise the importance of these codes in constructing meaning.

For example, consider the depiction of gender roles in literature. A structuralist analysis of female characters in 19th-century novels often reveals binary oppositions, such as virtuous versus fallen women, reflecting the rigid gender norms of the time. We can critique how such narratives reinforce or challenge societal expectations by identifying these patterns.

Similarly, semiotic analysis allows us to explore how cultural codes operate within texts. Consider the use of colours in literature: Red signifies passion or danger, while white symbolises purity or innocence.

These associations are not inherent but are shaped by cultural conventions. Analysing how authors manipulate these colour codes can reveal deeper layers of meaning within a text.

Moreover, cultural codes evolve, influencing how different generations interpret the same work. For instance, contemporary readers might approach Mary Shelley's "Frankenstein" through the lens of modern scientific ethics and technological anxieties. In contrast, early readers focused more on its Gothic elements and moral questions about creation and hubris. Understanding these shifts in interpretation highlights the dynamic interplay between text and reader, shaped by changing cultural contexts.

Poststructuralism and Deconstruction

Poststructuralism and Deconstruction: Unpacking Fluidity and Context in Literary Analysis Poststructuralism and deconstruction are critical frameworks introduced to challenge traditional interpretations of literature. These approaches emphasise the fluidity of meaning and the importance of context in literary analysis, providing readers with dynamic tools to dissect and understand texts from diverse angles.

Principles of Poststructuralism

Poststructuralism emerged as a reaction against the rigid structures posited by structuralism. Key figures like Jacques Derrida and Michel Foucault were instrumental in shaping this school of thought. Poststructuralism critiques the idea that language and structures can be understood as fixed entities. Instead, it argues that meanings are not stable but constantly shifting due to the interplay of various elements within language and society.

Derrida's notion of "decentering" is particularly significant. He argued that any text lacks a central, fixed meaning because language is unstable. This leads to the concept of difference, which suggests that words only acquire meaning through their differences from other words and not from any inherent qualities (Visit Profile, 2016). Similarly, Foucault focused on the power dynamics and discourses that shape knowledge and truth, asserting that what we consider 'truth' is influenced by historical and social contexts rather than an objective reality (*Post-Structuralism - an Overview | ScienceDirect Topics*, n.d.).

Introduction to Deconstruction

Deconstruction, as developed by Derrida, involves deconstructing texts to reveal internal contradictions and binary oppositions embedded within them. Binary oppositions are pairs of related terms or concepts that are opposite in meaning, such as good/evil, male/female, and presence/absence. These binaries often underpin our understanding of texts but also limit and simplify complex ideas.

One technique in deconstruction is "reading against the grain," where the critic identifies these binaries and subverts them to demonstrate their instability. For instance, Derrida's analysis often revealed how texts unconsciously undermine their stated intentions and meanings. In practical terms, this means examining a text closely to identify hidden biases, contradictions, and assumptions. Doing so can uncover alternative interpretations that challenge the dominant or surface readings.

Implications in Literary Analysis

The implications of poststructuralism and deconstruction for literary analysis are profound. They encourage readers to engage with texts more effectively and questioningly. Practical exercises can help students apply these theories. One such exercise is to take a canonical text and deliberately seek out passages that contradict its main themes or messages. For example, analysing a classic novel like "Pride and Prejudice" might involve exploring how characters' actions and dialogues sometimes subvert the very notions of class and gender norms that the text appears to endorse on the surface.

Another exercise could involve "intertextual reading," where students compare different texts to see how they inform or destabilise each other's meanings. This technique highlights how no text exists in isolation but is part of a broader network of cultural and textual influences.

Multiple Meanings

Understanding the multiplicity of meanings is another crucial aspect of poststructuralism and deconstruction. According to these theories, meaning is derived from the author's intent and the reader's interpretation, influenced by their unique context. This approach aligns with Roland Barthes' idea of the "Death of the Author," which proposes that the author's identity should not impose limits on the meanings derived from a text.

For instance, a poem written centuries ago may carry different meanings for contemporary readers based on their cultural and historical contexts. The text can be interpreted in multiple ways, highlighting the fluidity and contingency of meaning. This encourages readers to see texts as living entities that evolve and change over time, rather than static objects frozen in their original contexts.

Feminist Literary Criticism

Feminist Literary Criticism is a vital lens through which students can analyze and interpret literature. It offers insights into the ways gender dynamics and patriarchal structures shape texts. By examining the portrayal of women and the influence of gender in literary works, students can uncover deeper meanings and challenge traditional narratives.

Foundations of Feminist Criticism

The roots of Feminist Literary Criticism can be traced back to the early 20th century, with Virginia Woolf's seminal work "A Room of One's Own" serving as a cornerstone. Woolf argued for women's financial independence and intellectual freedom, setting the stage for future feminist critiques. This critical approach gained momentum during the second wave of feminism in the 1960s and 1970s, with scholars like Simone de Beauvoir and Elaine Showalter leading the charge.

Beauvoir's "The Second Sex" introduced the idea of women being perceived as "the Other," while Showalter's concept of "gynocriticism" focused on the study of women's writing from a female perspective. Over time, Feminist Literary Criticism has evolved to encompass diverse voices and perspectives, continually expanding its scope within literary studies (Brainly, 2024).

Key Concepts and Themes

Recurring themes such as patriarchy, identity, and representation are central to feminist literary criticism. Patriarchy refers to a social system where men hold primary power and dominate roles of political leadership, moral authority, and property control. This theme often manifests in literature through male-dominated narratives and the marginalisation of female characters. Critics analyse how texts reinforce or challenge patriarchal norms by examining character roles, plot structures, and language use.

Identity is another central theme, focusing on how gender shapes individuals' experiences and self-perceptions. Feminist critics explore how female characters navigate their identities in oppressive environments and how these struggles reflect broader societal issues. Representation involves scrutinising the ways women are depicted in literature. Are they portrayed as solid and complex individuals or reduced to stereotypes? This analysis helps reveal underlying biases and encourages more nuanced portrayals of women.

Practical Applications

Applying feminist frameworks to literary analysis can profoundly enhance understanding and interpretation. Here are some steps to consider when analysing texts through a feminist lens:

1. **Identify Gender Roles:** Examine the roles assigned to male and female characters. Are women depicted as passive or active agents? Do they have autonomy, or do male characters control them?

1. **Analyze Language and Imagery:** Pay attention to the language used to describe female characters. Is

Is it gendered or neutral? How do metaphors and symbols reinforce or challenge gender norms?

1. **Consider Authorial Intent:** Reflect on the author's background and potential biases. How might their gender and personal experiences influence their portrayal of female characters?

1. **Evaluate Power Dynamics:** Explore the relationships between male and female characters. Who holds power,

and how is it exercised? Are there instances of resistance or subversion of traditional gender roles?

By practising these steps, students can develop a critical eye for identifying patriarchal influences in literature and gain a deeper appreciation for feminist perspectives.

Intersectionality

Intersectionality, a term coined by Kimberlé Crenshaw, is essential for understanding how multiple identities intersect to shape individuals‘ experiences. It acknowledges that gender does not operate in isolation but is intertwined with other aspects of identity, such as race, class, sexuality, and ability. Feminist Literary Criticism benefits from an intersectional approach by recognising the complexity of characters' lives and the multifaceted nature of oppression.

For example, examining Toni Morrison's "Beloved" through an intersectional lens reveals how race and gender intersect to impact the protagonist's life. Sethe, the central character, is a formerly enslaved Black woman whose experiences of violence and trauma are compounded by her race and gender. Traditional feminist analyses may overlook the racial dimensions of her struggle, but an intersectional approach provides a more comprehensive understanding of her resilience and defiance against oppressive systems.

Marxist Theory and Literature

Marxist literary theory serves as a critical method for understanding how literature reflects and shapes societal narratives through the lens of class, ideology, and economic conditions. To begin with, it's essential to grasp the core concepts of Marxism that apply to literature. Central to Marxist thought is class struggle, the ongoing conflict between different social classes—primarily the bourgeoisie (owners of production) and the proletariat (working class). Karl Marx argued that human history is essentially a history of these class struggles, driven by material conditions and the distribution of resources. This foundational concept suggests that literature, like all cultural products, cannot be separated from its economic context and inherent power dynamics.

Another crucial concept in Marxism is ideology, which refers to the set of beliefs, values, and practices that support and justify the ruling class's interests. From a Marxist perspective, literature often perpetuates or challenges these ideologies. It can either reinforce the status quo by masking the realities of exploitation and inequality or unveil these contradictions to promote awareness and change. By examining literature through the prism of ideology, readers can unearth the hidden socio-economic messages embedded within texts.

In Marxist literary criticism, notable theorists such as Georg Lukács and Terry Eagleton have made significant contributions. Lukács emphasised the importance of historical context and realistic representation in literature, arguing that great works of art illuminate the socio-economic structures of their time. He believed that literature should reflect the complexities and contradictions of real life, offering readers a deeper understanding of societal forces at play. Similarly, Terry Eagleton has stressed literature's role in reflecting and shaping historical and material conditions. Eagleton's work often explores how literature can serve as a site of ideological struggle, revealing how texts negotiate, resist, or uphold dominant power structures.

To illustrate these theoretical concepts, we can turn to case studies and analysis of significant literary works. For instance, Charles Dickens's "Hard Times" can be analysed through a Marxist lens to uncover its critique of industrial capitalism. The novel portrays the harsh realities faced by workers in a factory town, highlighting the exploitation and dehumanisation inherent in the capitalist system. By focusing on the characters' struggles and the socio-economic environment, a Marxist reading of "Hard Times" reveals the underlying class conflicts and critiques the dominant ideologies of the time.

Similarly, George Orwell's "1984" can be examined to understand how totalitarian regimes use ideological control to maintain power. The novel depicts a dystopian society where the ruling Party manipulates language and information to suppress dissent and preserve dominance. Through the experiences of the protagonist, Winston Smith, Orwell exposes the mechanisms of ideological control and the importance of resisting oppressive systems. A Marxist analysis of "1984" sheds light on the interplay between economic conditions, ideology, and power, offering valuable insights into contemporary political and social issues.

Moving beyond classic literature, contemporary works also provide fertile ground for Marxist analysis. For example, Suzanne Collins's "The Hunger Games" series presents a dystopian world where the wealthy Capitol exploits and oppresses the impoverished districts. The series highlights the stark economic inequalities and the resulting class struggle, mirroring many aspects of modern society. By examining the dynamics of power, wealth, and resistance within the narrative, readers can apply Marxist theories to understand better the socio-economic issues depicted in the series.

The relevance of Marxist literary theory extends to contemporary literary criticism and modern society. Marxist theory offers valuable tools for analysing and critiquing literature in an era marked by increasing economic disparities and global capitalism. By foregrounding class and economic conditions issues, Marxist criticism encourages readers to question the status quo and consider alternative visions of society. It prompts us to think critically about how literature reflects and influences our understanding of social and economic realities.

Moreover, Marxist theory helps us recognise the ongoing relevance of class struggle in contemporary literature. Many modern works continue to address inequality, exploitation, and resistance issues, making Marxist analysis a robust framework for understanding these themes. For instance, novels like Mohsin Hamid's "The Reluctant Fundamentalist" and Aravind Adiga's "The White Tiger" explore the impact of globalisation, economic disparity, and social mobility on individuals and communities. By applying Marxist theories to these texts, readers can uncover the complex interplay between economic conditions and personal experiences.

Summary and Reflections

This chapter has explored the core principles of Formalism and New Criticism, two central methods in literary theory that focus on analysing a text's formal elements. We examined how scholars like John Crowe Ransom, Cleanth Brooks, and T.S. Eliot contributed to these schools of thought by emphasising the importance of examining literary devices, structure, and style.

Through examples like Shakespeare's "Sonnet 18" and Fitzgerald's "The Great Gatsby," we demonstrated how close readings of texts can reveal intricate layers of meaning without relying on external contexts such as the author's biography or historical background.

By learning about key concepts like the intentional fallacy and affective fallacy, students are equipped with tools to approach literature objectively, focusing solely on the text itself. This method fosters a deeper appreciation for the craft of writing but also encourages critical thinking and analytical skills. In classroom settings, applying these theories through close reading exercises helps students develop a structured approach to interpreting literature. Overall, this chapter provides a foundational understanding of analysing texts using Formalist and New Critic techniques, setting the stage for further exploration of literary theory.

Reference List

10.3: Formalism. (2019, December 12). Humanities LibreTexts. [https://human.libretexts.org/Bookshelves/ Literature_and_Literacy/Literacy_and_Critical_Thinking/ Writing_and_Critical_Thinking_Through_Literature_ (Ringo_and_Kashyap)/ 10%3A_About_Literary_Criticism/ 10.03%3A_Formalism](https://human.libretexts.org/ Bookshelves/Literature_and_Literacy/ Literacy_and_Critical_Thinking/ Writing_and_Critical_Thinking_Through_Literature_

(Ringo_and_Kashyap)/10%3A_About_Literary_Criticism/ 10.03%3A_Formalism)

Brainly. (2024). *Feminist literary criticism.* Retrieved from https://brainly.com/topic/english/feminist-literary-criticism

Chandler, D. (1994). *Semiotics for Beginners.* Web.pdx.edu. https://web.pdx.edu/~singlem/coursesite/ begsem.html

Feminist Literary Criticism: History, Example. (n.d.). Vaia. https://www.vaia.com/en-us/explanations/english-literature/literary-criticism-and-theory/feminist-literary-criticism/

Marxist Criticism. (2024). Wsu.edu. https://wsu.edu/~delahoyd/marxist.crit.html

Marxist Criticism | English 333. (n.d.). https://sites.wp.odu.edu/tatum-fisherengl333/theory-3/

New Criticism: Definition, Theory & Examples | Vaia. (2019). Vaia. https://www.vaia.com/en-us/explanations/ english-literature/literary-movements/new-criticism/

Post-Structuralism-anoverview|ScienceDirectTopics.(n.d.). Www.sciencedirect.com. https://www.sciencedirect.com/ topics/social-sciences/post-structuralism

Structuralism | Art and Literature Class Notes | Fiveable. (2024). Fiveable. me. https://library.fiveable.me/art-and-literature/unit-12/structuralism/study-guide/ iyqMGzmNsTiYY0pa

Visit profile. (2016, April 8). *My Guide to Literary Theory: Post-Structuralism/ Deconstruction.* Blogspot.com. http://achehir.blogspot.com/2016/04/my-guide-to-literary-theory-post.html

CHAPTER NINE

APPLYING CRITICAL THEORIES

"Applying critical theories to literary analysis opens a gateway to a deeper understanding and appreciation of texts. This chapter offers tools that allow readers to read and engage with literature through various critical lenses. By doing so, readers transform from passive consumers of stories into active participants in a dialogue with the text, uncovering layers of meaning that are otherwise hidden."

This chapter will explore methods for employing different critical theories in literary analysis. You will learn how to apply techniques such as close reading to dissect and interpret texts meticulously, paying attention to nuances in language, symbolism, and character perspectives. Additionally, we will delve into advanced strategies like contextual analysis to understand the influences of historical and cultural settings on a text. By the end of this chapter, you will be equipped with practical tools to engage with any piece of literature critically, enhancing your analytical skills and deepening your connection to the material.

Close Reading Techniques

Close reading is a powerful tool that allows students to delve deeply into texts and uncover nuanced meanings and themes. This process encourages readers to pay close attention to words' connotations and placement, which can significantly alter interpretation.

For instance, consider the difference between describing an old book as a "tome" versus just a "book." The word "tome" carries connotations of weightiness and historical significance, suggesting that the text may contain profound or scholarly material, whereas "book" is a more neutral term. Such subtle choices in diction invite readers to explore why certain words are chosen over others and what this reveals about the text (Source 2: *A Short Guide to Close Reading for Literary Analysis*, n.d.).

Symbols within a text often have layered meanings, making them crucial for holistic analysis. Take, for example, Robert Frost's poem "Design," in which a simple spider and flower become symbols rich with meaning. Closely reading such symbols requires looking beyond their surface-level representations to understand their profound significance and how they contribute to the text's theme. Symbols are not just decorative; they carry weight and meaning that enhance the reader's understanding of the literary work.

Understanding a character's perspective is another vital aspect of close reading. By immersing oneself in a character's viewpoint, readers can uncover inherent biases in storytelling. For instance, if a narrative describes events from the perspective of a wealthy protagonist, the depiction of poverty might be skewed or incomplete. Analysing these biases allows students to engage with the text critically and question the narrator's or characters' reliability.

Repetition within a text signifies importance, urging readers to explore why certain elements are emphasised. Repeated motifs or phrases can indicate underlying themes or highlight particular aspects of a character or setting that are critical to understanding the text. For instance, in many of Shakespeare's plays, the repetition of certain words or concepts, such as "honour" in "Julius Caesar," underscores central themes and prompts readers to consider their significance in different contexts.

To illustrate, imagine examining a passage where a character repeatedly refers to a seemingly mundane object, like a key. A close reading reveals that the key symbolises access to power or freedom, adding depth to the narrative. By paying attention to these repetitions, students can uncover layers of meaning that might otherwise be missed.

When engaging in close reading, it is essential to establish the text's readability and its purpose. Readability involves determining whether the language, signs, and symbols used in the text are understandable, while the purpose guides the reader's approach and the questions they pose to the text (Ane Ohrvik, 2024).

In the exploration phase, readers must delve into various text elements, such as its linguistic features, syntax, and thematic references. This phase is akin to putting the author's choices under a microscope, analysing the language's form, structure, and contextual significance. By doing so, readers gain insights into how the text operates at the micro and macro levels, revealing its complexities and nuances (Ane Ohrvik, 2024).

Consider the example of Robert Frost's poem "Design," where close reading involves examining the choice of words, imagery, and thematic elements. Words like "dimpled spider" and "white heal-all" invite readers to ponder the implications of these descriptions and how they contribute to the poem's overall eerie and contemplative mood. Such detailed analysis helps form a more comprehensive interpretation of the text.

As readers progress through the close reading process, they form questions and seek answers, thereby clarifying the text and giving it meaning. This iterative process helps refine interpretations and supports the development of well-informed literary analysis. Questioning and exploring the text fosters a deeper connection between the reader and the material, enhancing critical thinking skills (Source 2: *A Short Guide to Close Reading for Literary Analysis*, n.d.).

Furthermore, close reading also considers the historical and cultural contexts in which the text was created. While this aspect will be discussed in detail later in the chapter, it is worth noting that situating a text within its context can provide valuable insights into the author's motivations and the societal issues addressed in the work (Ane Ohrvik, 2024).

Understanding these contexts enriches the close reading experience by adding another layer of meaning to the analysis.

Contextual Analysis

Understanding a literary work's historical and cultural contexts is vital for deep and meaningful analysis. Literary texts do not exist in a vacuum; they are products of specific times, places, and cultures. By delving into these contexts, readers can uncover layers of meaning that might otherwise remain hidden.

Literary works often reflect or respond to their times' political, social, and cultural climates. For example, George Orwell's "1984," written after World War II, reflects the anxieties surrounding totalitarian regimes and the loss of individual freedoms. Similarly, Harper Lee's "To Kill a Mockingbird" offers a poignant critique of racial injustice in the American South during the 1930s. These works provide insights into the periods in which they were written and the broader societal concerns and issues that influenced their creation.

Historical context includes the social, religious, economic, and political conditions when the work was produced (Fleming, 2019). Understanding these factors can shed light on authorial intent and the societal critiques embedded within the text. For instance, Mary Shelley's "Frankenstein" cannot be fully appreciated without considering the Romantic movement and the Industrial Revolution's impact on Europe. The novel speaks to fears about unchecked technological advancement and its potential to dehumanise society—a theme that also resonates with contemporary readers.

Cultural context also plays a significant role in literary analysis. Cultural norms, values, and traditions inform the themes and messages authors wish to convey. In Charlotte Brontë's "Jane Eyre," the protagonist challenges the rigid social hierarchy and gender roles of Victorian England. Brontë's own experiences and observations of the limited opportunities available to women of her time heavily influence her portrayal of Jane as a strong, independent character seeking personal and financial autonomy (Twomey, 2016).

By examining the cultural context, readers can better understand how literary works address or reinforce prevailing cultural attitudes. For example, F. Scott Fitzgerald's "The Great Gatsby" captures the spirit of the Roaring Twenties in America—a period of excess, consumerism, and disillusionment. The novel critiques the American Dream, highlighting the moral decay that underpins the pursuit of wealth and status. Fitzgerald's life, marked by his tumultuous relationship with fame and fortune, further enriches our understanding of the text.

Authors' experiences often inform their storytelling and thematic choices. Personal history and broader historical and cultural contexts can shape an author's perspective and the subjects they choose to explore. James Joyce's "Ulysses," set in Dublin on June 16, 1904, draws heavily from Joyce's own life experiences and the socio-political landscape of Ireland. The novel's stream-of-consciousness technique and exploration of everyday life exemplify modernist concerns with capturing the complexities of human thought and experience.

Guidelines for incorporating historical and cultural contexts into literary analysis include researching the period in which a work was written, considering the author's background and personal experiences, and examining how societal values and events may have influenced the text. For instance, when analysing Toni Morrison's "Beloved," it is essential to understand the historical context of slavery in America and the cultural memory of African American communities. Morrison's dedication to preserving African American history and experience informs the novel's exploration of trauma and resilience.

Similarly, understanding the myths and cultural narratives that influence a work can enhance its interpretation. Aeschylus' "Agamemnon," written in ancient Greece, cannot be fully grasped without knowledge of Greek mythology and the cultural significance of the Trojan War. This context helps readers appreciate the play's exploration of themes such as fate, justice, and the human condition.

Intertextual connections offer another layer of analysis in addition to historical and cultural contexts. Authors often engage with existing texts by drawing inspiration or challenging previous works.

For example, T.S. Eliot's "The Waste Land" is rich with references to classical literature, religious texts, and contemporary works. Recognising these allusions and their significance within the poem enhances our understanding of Eliot's critique of post-World War I society.

Finally, it is essential to note that historical and cultural contexts are dynamic and multifaceted. They encompass various aspects of human life, including social norms, political ideologies, economic conditions, and cultural practices. When analysing a text, adopting a holistic approach that considers multiple perspectives and influences is beneficial. This enriches the analysis and provides a more comprehensive understanding of the work's place within its historical and cultural milieu.

Intertextuality and Comparative Studies

Exploring connections between texts provides profound insights into the nature of literature and human experience. This subpoint emphasises the importance of intertextuality, comparative analysis, shared themes, and the influence of different genres, enriching understanding through comparison.

Firstly, intertextuality is a significant concept in literary analysis, positing that no text exists in isolation. Every piece of writing is part of a broader scholarly conversation, influenced by, and in turn influencing, other works. By examining how texts relate, students can uncover deeper meanings and connections. For example, Margaret Atwood's "Oryx and Crake" engages in dialogue with works like George Orwell's "1984" and Aldous Huxley's "Brave New World," each exploring dystopian futures shaped by societal anxieties about technology and control (*Intertex tuality: Connecting Texts*, n.d.).

The practice of comparative analysis enriches critical thinking, urging students to consider authorial choices and thematic explorations across different works. Students who compare texts scrutinise how authors handle similar themes or narrative strategies. This exercise sharpens analytical skills as students evaluate why an author might choose one approach over another, what themes are prioritised, and how these choices impact the reader's understanding. For instance, comparing the treatment of war in Erich Maria Remarque's "All Quiet on the Western Front" with Wilfred Owen's war poetry highlights differing perspectives on conflict's brutality and futility. As students juxtapose these works, they gain insight into the varied ways literature can present and critique real-world issues.

Discussing shared themes among texts allows students to engage with universal human experiences. Literature often revolves around recurring themes such as love, power, death, and identity. Students develop a more comprehensive understanding of the human condition by examining how different authors and cultures address these themes. For example, the theme of forbidden love in Shakespeare's "Romeo and Juliet" and Emily Bronte's "Wuthering Heights" illustrates how different periods and social contexts shape narratives around similar emotional experiences. Such comparisons enable students to see how everyday human struggles transcend cultural and temporal boundaries.

Different genres also facilitate unique authorial strategies, affecting reader engagement and interpretation. Each genre—drama, satire, or science fiction—comes with its conventions and techniques, offering distinct lenses through which to view and analyse texts. For instance, the irony and exaggeration in Jonathan Swift's "A Modest Proposal" starkly contrast with the realism and sombre tone in Toni Morrison's "Beloved." Understanding genre-specific strategies helps students appreciate the diverse ways authors construct meaning and elicit audience responses. This awareness encourages flexibility in reading and interpreting texts across different literary forms.

By integrating these points, exploring connections between texts using intertextuality, comparative analysis of shared themes, and genre influences enhances comprehension and cultivates a richer appreciation of literature. Intertextuality reveals how texts converse with each other, contributing to an ongoing literary dialogue. Comparative analysis hones critical thinking by examining authorial decisions and thematic development. Discussing shared themes connects students to universal experiences, fostering empathy and a broader worldview. Finally, an awareness of genre differences highlights the versatility of literary expression, promoting a deeper engagement with texts.

Educators and students can employ several practical strategies to apply these concepts effectively. One method is to create thematic units where multiple texts addressing similar themes are studied together. For example, a unit on the theme of rebellion might include George Orwell's "1984," Alan Moore's "V for Vendetta," and Suzanne Collins' "The Hunger Games". Comparing these works would help students explore different portrayals of resistance against oppressive systems and the varying narrative techniques employed.

Another approach involves focusing on the authorial style and technique. Students could compare how writers use symbolism, character development, or narrative structure to convey their themes. A comparative analysis of symbolism might involve examining water use in T.S. Eliot's "The Waste Land" versus its use in Jean Rhys' "Wide Sargasso Sea." Such assignments encourage students to delve into the nuances of literary devices and their effects on interpretation.

Encouraging students to explore texts from diverse cultural backgrounds also broadens their literary horizons. Assignments that pair Western canonical works with non-Western literature can reveal fascinating contrasts and similarities. For instance, comparing Chinua Achebe's "Things Fall Apart" with Joseph Conrad's "Heart of Darkness" offers insights into colonialism's impact from both the colonised and coloniser's perspectives. These cross-cultural comparisons deepen students' understanding of global literary traditions and perspectives.

Moreover, incorporating multimedia and contemporary texts alongside traditional literature can make these explorations more engaging. Integrating film adaptations, graphic novels, or digital storytelling allows students to see how themes and narratives are adapted across different media. For instance, analysing the portrayal of heroism in the original texts and film adaptations of "The Lord of the Rings" can illustrate how visual and textual elements contribute to storytelling.

Reader-Response Criticism

In exploring how readers' interpretations impact the meaning of a literary work, it's essential to understand that subjective analysis plays a vital role. Reader-response theory posits that meaning is not solely derived from the text but is shaped by the reader's experiences, emotions, and personal history (Long, 2024). This perspective shifts the focus from authorial intent and textual analysis to the interactive experience between the reader and the text.

Reader-response theory suggests that every individual brings unique life experiences and cultural backgrounds to their reading, profoundly influencing their interpretation. For instance, a reader who has experienced loss may connect deeply with themes of grief in a novel, interpreting characters' actions and dialogues through the lens of their own emotions. This personal connection can reveal layers of meaning that might remain hidden in a more objective analysis.

Social identities and cultures also play a crucial role in shaping collective readings and discussions of texts. A diverse group of readers might generate a wide range of interpretations based on their ethnic, gender, or socio-economic backgrounds. These differences highlight the multiplicity of meanings a single text can hold and emphasize the importance of considering varied perspectives in literary analysis. For example, feminist and postcolonial readings often bring forward aspects of power dynamics and marginalization that others might overlook.

Specific narrative elements such as empathy, nostalgia, or discomfort can invoke strong emotional responses. A well-rounded character facing moral dilemmas can evoke empathy in readers, making them reflect on their ethical beliefs and choices. Similarly, settings and plot events that resonate with readers' past experiences can stir feelings of nostalgia. Conversely, challenging themes like injustice or trauma can evoke discomfort, prompting readers to confront complex societal issues through the safety of the fictional world.

Literature encourages multiple perspectives, thereby enhancing discussions among students. Inviting students to share their personal interpretations fosters a richer classroom dialogue where differing views are examined and respected. This process not only aids in developing critical thinking skills but also leads to a more comprehensive understanding of the text. For instance, discussing Harper Lee's "To Kill a Mockingbird" might lead to varied insights into racial injustice and moral courage, each influenced by the readers' histories and values.

The concept of the implied reader further emphasises the interaction between text and reader. The implied reader is an idealised version of the audience that the text seems to address, shaped by the text's style, tone, and themes (6.3: Focus on Reader-Response Strategies, 2019). This notion acknowledges that authors often have a specific target audience, intending their work to be interpreted in particular ways. However, actual readers may deviate from this intended pathway, bringing their subjectivity into play.

Engaging with a text through receptor reader response involves setting aside preconceptions and entering a state of empathetic engagement with the narrative. Here, readers attune themselves to the text's language, tone, and style, striving to understand it on its own terms rather than imposing their viewpoints. This approach highlights the diversity of responses a single text can generate and underscores the significance of individual subjectivity in literary interpretation.

The practice of subjective reader response is particularly relevant in educational settings, where students learn to recognise and value their interpretations alongside traditional analyses. Students can track their evolving perspectives and engage deeply with the text by writing down their thoughts and reactions in journals or annotations. Comparing these personal reflections with established interpretations enhances their analytical skills and broadens their understanding of literature.

Guidelines for practising subjective reader response include reading the text closely, reflecting on one's experiences about the narrative, noting initial thoughts and reactions, sharing interpretations with peers, and finally, reflecting on how personal experiences influenced one's reading. This structured approach ensures that students approach texts both personally and critically.

The goal of subjective reader response is to appreciate the co-creative process between reader and text. Readers are not passive recipients of information; they construct meaning through their interactions with the narrative. This dynamic relationship enriches the reading experience and allows literature to resonate personally, fostering a deeper connection with the text.

Applying Psychoanalytic Theory

Psychoanalytic theory offers a powerful lens through which to analyse literary texts, revealing hidden meanings and complex character dynamics. By applying this theory, readers can uncover deeper psychological motivations in characters, understand intricate plot developments, and gain insights into the unconscious contributions of authors themselves.

One of the fundamental aspects of psychoanalytic theory is its emphasis on Freudian perspectives.

Sigmund Freud's theories suggest that human behaviour stems from unconscious desires and unresolved conflicts. Freudian analysis can shed light on character motivations in literature by examining these subconscious drivers. For instance, a character's seemingly irrational actions may reveal underlying fears or desires, offering a more nuanced understanding of their behaviour. This approach can also highlight repressed emotions and thoughts that might not be immediately apparent through surface-level reading.

Freud's model divides the mind into the Id, Ego, and Superego. The Id embodies primal instincts and desires, operating on a pleasure principle without concern for societal norms. The Ego, governed by reality, mediates between the Id's desires and societal demands. The Superego represents internalised moral standards and ideals. Balancing these three elements can provide valuable insights into character conflicts and resolutions within literary works. For example, a protagonist's struggle to choose between forbidden desires (Id) and societal expectations (Superego), managed by their rational decision-making (Ego), can create intense internal and external conflicts, driving the plot forward. Recognising these dynamics helps readers understand why characters act as they do and how these actions contribute to the story's progression.

Dreams and dream-like sequences in literature often serve as windows into the unconscious mind. According to Freud, dreams are manifestations of our deepest desires and fears. In literary analysis, examining such sequences can reveal the underlying tensions within characters. For instance, if a character repeatedly dreams of drowning, it could symbolise overwhelming anxiety or feelings of being trapped. These dreams provide clues about the character's psyche and may foreshadow future events or resolutions in the narrative. Exploring these dreamscapes enriches the reading experience, allowing readers to connect more deeply with the characters' inner lives.

Authors' personal struggles and intentions also play a significant role in psychoanalytic literary criticism. Freud believed an author's work could be seen as an extension of their unconscious mind, reflecting personal conflicts and desires. By delving into authors' backgrounds and considering their life experiences, readers can uncover additional layers of meaning in their texts. For example, analysing Virginia Woolf's "Mrs. Dalloway" through the lens of her known struggles with mental illness adds depth to the portrayal of the protagonist's psychological landscape. This perspective allows readers to understand how an author's fears, hopes, and traumas inform their creative process, thus enriching the literary analysis.

It is crucial to develop a systematic approach to harness the power of psychoanalytic theory in literary analysis effectively. When exploring character motivations through a Freudian perspective, begin by identifying key actions or decisions made by the characters. Consider what unconscious desires or conflicts might drive these behaviours. Look for symbols, recurring themes, or patterns that hint at repressed emotions. By piecing together these elements, readers can construct a more comprehensive picture of the character's psychological makeup.

Incorporating the concepts of Id, Ego, and Superego requires careful examination of the text to identify moments where these components come into play. Please pay attention to scenes of conflict or decision-making, noting how characters navigate their primal desires, societal expectations, and moral imperatives. Analysing these interactions can offer insights into the overall theme and message of the work.

Dream sequences should be scrutinised for symbolic content and emotional undertones. What imagery stands out? How do these dreams relate to the character's waking life? Connecting the fantastical elements of dreams to real-life anxieties or desires can unlock hidden meanings and add depth to the analysis.

Understanding authorial intent involves researching the author's biography and looking for parallels between their life experiences and the themes or characters in their work. However, while considering the authorial background, it is essential to balance this with the text to avoid overemphasising biographical interpretation. The goal is to use the author's experiences as one of many tools to deepen the understanding of the text.

Summary and Reflections

This chapter has thoroughly explored methods for employing critical theories in literary analysis. By examining close reading techniques, we learned to delve deeply into texts to uncover nuanced meanings and themes. We also discussed the importance of understanding historical and cultural contexts to enrich our interpretations and highlighted the value of intertextuality and comparative studies in drawing connections between different works. Each strategy equips students with practical tools to engage more profoundly with literature.

As we conclude, it is essential to recognise that the critical theories and strategies introduced here offer a robust framework for literary analysis. These approaches encourage readers to look beyond surface-level interpretations and consider more profound, more complex layers within texts. Whether analysing symbols, understanding character perspectives, or exploring contextual backgrounds, these techniques foster a richer appreciation of literature. Integrating these methods will enhance your ability to engage with texts and develop insightful analyses critically.

Reference List

6.3: Focus on Reader-Response Strategies. (2019, August 16). Humanities LibreTexts. https://human.libretexts.org/Bookshelves/Literature_and_Literacy/Literacy_and_Critical_Thinking/Creating_Literary_Analysis/

6%3A_Writing_about_Readers_-_Applying_Reader-Response_Theory/
6.03%3A_Focus_on_Reader-Response_Strategies

A Short Guide to Close Reading for Literary Analysis. (n.d.). The Writing Center. https://writing.wisc.edu/handbook/closereading/

Ane Ohrvik. (2024, April 24). *What is close reading? An exploration of a methodology.* Rethinking History; Taylor & Francis. https://doi.org/10.1080/13642529.2024.2345001

English A: Lang Lit: Intertextuality: connecting texts. (2015). Philpot. education. https://philpot.education/mod/page/view.php?id=89

Fleming, G. (2019, August 19). *Understanding Historic Context Is Key to Analysis and Interpretation.* ThoughtCo. https://www.thoughtco.com/what-is-historical-context-1857069

Intertextuality: Connecting Texts. (n.d.). MRS. H'S IB ENGLISH LANGUAGE and LITERATURE. https://hernandeziblangandlit.weebly.com/intertextuality-connecting-texts.html

Long, L. (2024). *What Is Reader Response?* Cwi.pressbooks.pub. https://cwi.pressbooks.pub/lit-crit/chapter/what-is-reader-response/

Nash, J. (2018, May 7). *Psychoanalysis: A Brief History of Freud's Psychoanalytic Theory [2019].* PositivePsychology.com. https://positivepsychology.com/psychoanalysis/

Psychoanalytic Literary Criticism: Definition. (n.d.). Vaia. https://www.vaia.com/en-us/explanations/english-literature/literary-criticism-and-theory/psychoanalytic-literary-criticism/

Twomey, E. (2016, June 2). *The Importance of Context in Literature.* Www.vcestudyguides.com.

https://www.vcestudyguides.com/blog/the-importance-of-context-in-literature

CHAPTER TEN

RESEARCH AND WRITING IN LITERATURE

Research and writing in literature studies are essential skills for any student or scholar aiming to excel in the field. These processes demand an understanding of how to gather and evaluate sources and the ability to articulate insights through well-structured essays. Effective research enables students to build a foundation of credible information, while proficient writing helps convey their analyses with clarity and precision. This chapter focuses on equipping students with these foundational skills, guiding them from the initial stages of research to the finer points of composing and refining their literary essays.

This chapter explores methods for conducting thorough and credible literary research. It begins by identifying reliable sources, differentiating between scholarly articles and general sources, and developing meaningful research questions. Then, the chapter delves into integrating literary theory to enhance analysis, organising research findings efficiently, and managing the collected materials effectively.

Furthermore, it guides structuring and writing literary essays, emphasising evidence-based arguments, critical thinking, and literary devices. Readers will also learn the importance of editing and revising drafts to produce polished final essays. By the end of the chapter, students will be well-prepared to navigate the complexities of literary research and composition, ultimately enhancing their academic and professional pursuits.

Conducting Literary Research

In literary studies, conducting effective research requires specialised skills tailored to the field's unique demands. One crucial aspect is identifying reliable sources. Differentiating between scholarly, peer-reviewed articles and general sources is essential for maintaining academic credibility. Scholarly articles undergo rigorous review by experts in the field before publication, ensuring their reliability and relevance. In contrast, general sources, such as blog posts or opinion pieces, may need more scrutiny and can often present biased or unfounded information. To ensure high-quality research, students should prioritise scholarly sources to build a solid foundation for their work.

Developing meaningful research questions is another vital skill in literature studies. Formulating focused and insightful questions helps guide the research process and narrows the vast available resources. Practical research questions are specific, manageable, and relevant to the topic. For instance, instead of asking a broad question like, "What is the significance of symbolism in literature?" a more focused question would be, "How does the use of symbolism in Nathaniel Hawthorne's 'The Scarlet Letter' enhance the novel's themes of sin and redemption?" This specificity allows for a more targeted approach to gathering and analysing data.

Integrating literary theory into research enriches the analysis and provides deeper insights into texts. Literary theories, such as feminism, Marxism, psychoanalysis, and postcolonialism, offer diverse lenses through which literature can be interpreted. For example, using feminist theory to examine Charlotte Brontë's "Jane Eyre" can shed light on gender dynamics and the social constraints faced by women during the Victorian era. Incorporating these theoretical frameworks not only broadens the scope of research but also enhances the critical analysis of literary works.

Organising research findings efficiently is crucial for managing the resources collected during the research process. One effective strategy is to categorise sources based on themes or topics. Creating annotated bibliographies, where summaries and evaluations of each source are included, can also help track critical points and arguments. Additionally, digital tools such as reference management software (e.g., Zotero or EndNote) can streamline the organisation and citation process. These tools allow students to store, categorise, and cite sources effortlessly, reducing the risk of losing important information.

Identifying reliable sources is paramount in literary research. Scholarly, peer-reviewed articles provide a wealth of validated knowledge, whereas general sources may need more rigour. Peer-reviewed journals, books published by reputable academic presses, and conference proceedings are typical examples of credible sources. Accessing these through university libraries and academic databases like JSTOR or Google Scholar is advisable. Using non-scholarly sources should be limited to instances where they provide unique perspectives or primary data that cannot be found elsewhere. This discerning approach ensures that the research is built on a sound foundation of academic integrity.

Formulating precise and insightful research questions plays a significant role in guiding the research journey. An effective research question should be clear, focused, and researchable within the given constraints. Asking open-ended questions that probe into a literary text's "how" and "why" aspects can yield richer analysis. For example, rather than asking, "Is 'Frankenstein' a critique of science?" a more insightful question might be, "How does Mary Shelley's 'Frankenstein' reflect contemporary anxieties about scientific exploration and ethical responsibility?" Such questions lead to more substantial, analytical research and contribute to a more engaging and nuanced essay.

Incorporating literary theory into research adds depth and perspective to literary analysis. Theories provide frameworks that can reveal hidden meanings or societal implications within texts. For instance, applying psychoanalytic theory to William Shakespeare's "Hamlet" might explore the protagonist's Oedipal complex, while a Marxist approach could analyse class struggles depicted in Charles Dickens's "Great Expectations." However, it's essential to use theories judiciously, ensuring that the chosen framework genuinely enhances the understanding of the text rather than forcing an unwarranted interpretation. Properly applied, literary theory can illuminate new dimensions of even familiar works, enriching both the research process and its outcomes.

Efficiently managing research materials is indispensable for ensuring that all gathered information is accessible and usable when needed. One practical method is to divide research notes into thematic categories corresponding to parts of the research question. Another technique is maintaining a detailed research journal, documenting the rationale behind selecting particular sources and noting reflections on how they contribute to the overall argument. Utilising digital tools for creating mind maps or concept maps can visually organise connections between ideas and sources, making it easier to structure the final paper cohesively. By systematically organising research findings, students can streamline the writing process, reduce redundancy, and craft well-supported arguments more easily.

Writing Literary Essays

A literary essay allows students to engage deeply with a text, proposing insightful analyses and developing critical perspectives. To accomplish this, several essential components must be mastered.

Structuring the Essay

Understanding the typical structure of a literary essay is foundational. A well-structured essay guides the reader through your analysis logically and coherently. Generally, a literary essay consists of an introduction, body paragraphs, and a conclusion.

Introduction: The introduction should provide background information about the analysed text and present a clear thesis statement. This thesis is the central argument or interpretation of the entire essay. It should be concise, compelling, and reflective of the following analysis.

Body Paragraphs: Each body paragraph should focus on a specific aspect of the text that supports your thesis. Start each paragraph with a topic sentence that introduces the main idea. Follow this with textual evidence—quotes or detailed references to the text—and an analysis that explains how this evidence supports your thesis. Connect each paragraph to your main argument to maintain coherence throughout the essay.

Conclusion: Summarize the main points discussed in the body paragraphs and restate the thesis in a new light, considering the insights gained from the analysis. Avoid introducing new information in the conclusion; instead, focus on reinforcing the significance of your study and its broader implications.

Developing Arguments

Crafting solid arguments backed by textual evidence is crucial in literary essays. An argument should be more than a statement of opinion; it must be supported by concrete evidence from the text.

Evidence-Based Analysis: Use quotes and specific examples from the text to bolster your arguments. For instance, if your thesis claims that a particular character symbolises freedom, provide passages where the character's actions, dialogue, or descriptions support this interpretation. Ensure that your evidence is relevant and connected to your argument.

Critical Thinking: Engage critically with the text, questioning and interpreting the author's choices.

Consider alternative interpretations and address potential counterarguments. This depth of analysis demonstrates your ability to think critically and enhances the persuasiveness of your essay.

Incorporating Literary Devices

Utilising literary terms and analysis in essays can deepen your engagement with the text and enrich your analysis. Literary devices such as symbolism, metaphor, imagery, and irony are tools that authors use to add layers of meaning to their work.

Symbolism and Metaphor: Identify and analyse symbols and metaphors within the text. Explain what they represent and how they contribute to the themes or messages of the work. For instance, if a recurring image of birds appears in a novel, explore what the birds might symbolise and how this symbolism affects your understanding of the text.

Imagery and Irony: Pay attention to the author's use of imagery and irony. Describe how these devices create mood, highlight themes, or reveal character traits. By incorporating discussions of literary devices into your essay, you demonstrate a nuanced understanding of the text and provide a richer analysis.

Editing and Revising

Editing and revising are essential for refining drafts into polished essays. Initial drafts often contain errors, unclear passages, or underdeveloped arguments that must be addressed before final submission.

Self-Editing Techniques: Begin by reading your essay aloud to catch awkward phrasing or grammatical errors. Check for clarity and coherence, ensuring that each paragraph logically flows to the next and effectively supports your thesis. Look for areas where you can tighten your prose by eliminating unnecessary words or repetitive statements.

Peer Review: If possible, have peers review your essay. Fresh eyes can provide valuable feedback on the strengths and weaknesses of your analysis. They might point out confusing sections, offer suggestions for improving your arguments, or notice errors you overlooked.

Refinement: Based on feedback, revise your essay to enhance clarity, coherence, and depth of analysis.

Focus on strengthening your arguments, improving transitions between paragraphs, and ensuring your thesis is consistently supported throughout the essay. Additionally, double-check your citations to ensure they are accurate and properly formatted.

Avoiding Plagiarism

In academic writing, understanding plagiarism is essential for maintaining integrity in one's work.

Plagiarism occurs when someone presents another person's ideas, words, or creations as their own without giving proper credit. This can include copying text, paraphrasing without acknowledgement, and even reusing one's previous work (self-plagiarism) without citation. Plagiarism fundamentally undermines learning, preventing proper comprehension and original thought from developing. Upholding integrity is crucial for institutions to produce ethical, critical thinkers who can contribute meaningfully to their fields.

One of the best ways to avoid plagiarism is by properly attributing sources. Proper attribution means acknowledging the source of any information, idea, or data used in your writing. By doing this, you give credit to the creators and help maintain transparency and trust in academic work. Students should familiarise themselves with citation guidelines and ensure they apply them consistently. Every direct quote, idea, theory, or data that is not common knowledge must be cited correctly.

To make sure each source is attributed correctly, follow these practices:

1. Use quotation marks for direct quotes and cite the original author, year, and page number.
2. When paraphrasing, rewrite the original idea in your own words and still cite the author and year.
3. Create a detailed bibliography with full publication details for all references used.

Citation management tools like Zotero can significantly aid in organising and citing sources properly.

Utilising plagiarism checkers is another effective strategy for ensuring originality in your work. Plagiarism detection software like iThenticate analyses documents by comparing them against extensive databases of existing works. These tools highlight passages that match other texts, allowing writers to identify and address potential issues before submission. Features of these tools often include detailed reports that outline areas with significant overlap and suggestions for proper citation. Using these tools, students can proactively ensure their papers are free from unintentional plagiarism and uphold academic standards.

Building originality through research is equally important in academic writing. Genuine research involves more than just reading and summarising existing literature; it requires synthesising various perspectives to develop new insights. To encourage original thought, students should:

- Paraphrase content in their own words instead of copying verbatim passages.
- Note key ideas using bullet points or keywords rather than complete sentences.

- Capture original reactions, analysis, and insights during research.

These methods help prevent reliance on regurgitating source material and foster deeper understanding and unique contributions to the topic.

It is vital to integrate sources with original commentary seamlessly during the drafting process. Drafting academic pieces should involve weaving in paraphrased content from sources to support original analysis while using direct quotes sparingly to emphasise key points. Synthesising multiple perspectives helps develop well-rounded arguments and conclusions that reflect the writer's analytical capabilities. Carefully self-editing drafts to confirm the originality and proper integration of external research are also necessary.

Self-editing steps include:

1. Running plagiarism checks using tools like iThenticate.
2. Verifying that all sources are correctly cited.
3. Scrutinizing the integration of external research and reworking where needed.
4. Reflecting critically on how different sources combine with personal insights to ensure authenticity.

Understanding what constitutes "common knowledge" versus what needs citation is another aspect of avoiding plagiarism. Common knowledge refers to widely accepted and known information by a large audience, which typically does not require citation. In contrast, specific claims, statistics, theories, and findings must be credited to their sources. When in doubt, it is always safer to provide a citation to avoid accidental plagiarism.

Educators play a crucial role in helping students navigate these ethical considerations. Institutions can support students by hosting workshops on academic integrity and proper citation methods. Guest speakers can underscore the significance of intellectual property and the consequences of plagiarism in both academic and professional settings. Refresher tutorials before major assessments can also reinforce these principles. Additionally, online training tools for self-paced learning around academic writing best practices can be beneficial.

Maintaining open communication about writing uncertainties and providing resources like campus writing centres further support students in developing ethical writing habits. Writing centres can offer personalised assistance, ensuring students understand how to correctly attribute sources and formulate original ideas.

Citing Sources Accurately

Accurate citation practices are foundational to literary research and writing. They appropriately credit the original authors and foster a more profound respect for intellectual property. This section explores various aspects of citation practices, including understanding different citation styles, integrating citations effectively within texts, creating works cited or reference pages, and using tools to manage citations.

Understanding Citation Styles:

Different disciplines in literary studies may require different citation styles. The most common formats include MLA (Modern Language Association), APA (American Psychological Association), and Chicago. Each has specific rules for formatting citations and creating bibliographies.

MLA is often used in humanities, particularly literature, and focuses on the author-page format. For example, an in-text citation in MLA format might look like this: (Langer 1527). The full citation would appear on the Works Cited page as Langer, R. "New Methods of Drug Delivery." Science, vol. 249, no. 4976, 1990, pp. 1527-1533.

APA is used mainly in social sciences and follows an author-date-page format. An APA in-text citation might read: (Langer, 1990, p. 1527). On the References page, it would be detailed thus: Langer, R. (1990). New methods of drug delivery. Science, 249(4976), 1527-1533.

Chicago style offers two systems: notes and bibliography, favoured in history and the humanities, and author-date, used in physical, natural, and social sciences. The notes and bibliography method uses footnotes or endnotes along with a bibliography. A sample note would be R. Langer, "New Methods of Drug Delivery," Science 249, no. 4976 (1990): 1527-33. This citation in a bibliography will read Langer, R. "New Methods of Drug Delivery." Science 249, no. 4976 (1990): 1527-33.

Effective Citation Practices:

Integrating citations within the text involves smoothly embedding them in your narrative to support your arguments. Citations can enhance credibility and provide evidence for claims. Transition phrases such as "according to," "as stated by," and "in the words of" can help merge citations into sentences without interrupting the flow. For instance, using an MLA citation, you might write: According to Langer, the new methods of drug delivery have significant potential (1527). This sentence incorporates the citation naturally, offering proof without disrupting readability.

Creating Works Cited or Reference Pages: Compiling bibliographies at the end of your paper is crucial for tracking down the sources you used and allowing readers to find the original work. In MLA, this section is titled "Works Cited" and lists all sources referenced alphabetically by the author's last name. APA names this section "References," while Chicago uses either "Bibliography" or "References," depending on the specific system employed.

For example, In MLA:

Works Cited:

Langer, R. "New Methods of Drug Delivery." Science, vol. 249, no. 4976, 1990, pp. 1527-1533.

In APA:

References:

Langer, R. (1990). New methods of drug delivery. Science, 249(4976), 1527-1533.

In Chicago: Bibliography:

Langer, R. "New Methods of Drug Delivery." Science 249, no. 4976 (1990): 1527-1533.

Using Citation Management Tools:

Various tools can assist in managing citations, making the process more efficient and less error-prone. Tools like EndNote, Zotero, and Mendeley help organise research materials, generate citations, and create bibliographies automatically.

EndNote is a software tool for publishing and managing bibliographies, citations, and references. It offers advanced features such as group references and search capabilities across multiple databases.

Zotero is free, open-source software that helps collect, organise, cite, and share research. It captures research material from databases and websites and stores it in a library that can be searched and organised efficiently.

Mendeley combines desktop and web-based applications, providing tools for reference management and social collaboration. It enables users to import papers, manage PDFs, and collaborate online with other researchers.

Proper citation management tools ensure accuracy and save time. These tools generate formatted citations and bibliographies by inputting details once, reducing the risk of human error.

Conclusion Preparing for Publication

Preparing literary work for publication can be an intricate process laden with challenges and opportunities. Understanding how to navigate this terrain is essential for students who want their hard work recognized and disseminated. This subpoint explores the crucial steps in preparing work for publication, focusing on identifying suitable venues, drafting cover letters, navigating the review process, and marketing and promoting published work.

Identifying Suitable Venues

Choosing the right venue to submit your literary work is the first critical step in publication. Identifying a suitable journal, magazine, or platform requires understanding the nature of your work and matching it to the appropriate audience. For academic journals, the Think. Check. Submit. Initiative provides invaluable tools for evaluating whether a journal is trustworthy (*How to Write a Journal Article - Tips and Structure Guide*, n.d.). Additionally, reviewing a journal's aims and scope helps ensure your article aligns with what the journal seeks to accomplish.

To determine the best fit, conduct a thorough search within your field. Examine various publications, look at their recent issues, and note the types of articles they feature. This will provide insights into the publication's focus and preferred topics. Don't hesitate to ask mentors or colleagues for recommendations, as their experiences can guide you toward reputable venues. Remember, submitting to a well-matched publication increases the chances of acceptance and ensures your work reaches the right audience.

Drafting Cover Letters

An effective cover letter can significantly impact the success of your submission. It serves as your first communication with the editor and presents an opportunity to make a strong impression. A well-crafted cover letter should be succinct, professional, and tailored to the publication.

Begin by addressing the editor by name, if possible. Introduce yourself and briefly describe your credentials and affiliation. Then, provide a concise summary of your manuscript, highlighting its importance, originality, and why it's a good fit for the journal. Mention if you've cited any works previously published in that journal, as this demonstrates familiarity with and relevance to their content.

Clearly state any competing interests and declare that the work hasn't been submitted elsewhere simultaneously. End with a courteous closing, expressing your hope for a favourable consideration and thanking the editor for their time. Practising professionalism and clarity in your cover letter sets the stage for a successful communication channel with the editors (*How to Write a Journal Article - Tips and Structure Guide*, n.d.).

Navigating the Review Process

Understanding the editorial workflow is crucial in navigating the review process smoothly. Once your manuscript is submitted, the editor typically undergoes an initial screening to ensure it fits the journal's scope and standards. If it passes this stage, it is sent out for peer review, where experts assess its validity, originality, and significance.

The review process can be lengthy and may involve several revisions based on reviewer feedback. Be prepared to receive constructive criticism and use it to improve your manuscript. Address each comment thoughtfully, making the necessary changes or providing justified explanations for not incorporating specific suggestions.

Maintaining a positive attitude and showing a willingness to collaborate goes a long way during this phase. Revisions are a normal part of the publication journey and contribute to enhancing the quality of your work. Respond promptly to editorial queries and meet all deadlines to ensure a smooth and efficient review process.

Marketing and Promoting Published Work

Once your work is published, the next step is to ensure it reaches a broader audience. Effective marketing and promotion are critical for increasing the visibility and impact of your published work. Start by sharing your publication on social media platforms frequented by your target audience. Draft engaging posts highlighting your work's key findings and significance, using hashtags relevant to your field to reach a wider community.

Consider creating a personal or professional website to showcase your published papers and ongoing research projects. This is a central hub for your academic portfolio, making it easier for others to find and reference your work. Additionally, leverage email newsletters to inform your network about your latest publications and achievements.

Engaging with the academic community also plays a significant role in promoting your work. Attend conferences, webinars, and workshops where you can present your findings, discuss your research with peers, and build connections. Collaborations and discussions at these events often lead to citations and further dissemination of your work.

Moreover, consider writing accessible summaries of your research for general audiences, such as blog posts or opinion pieces for popular science magazines. These summaries help bridge the gap between academia and the public, making your findings more understandable and impactful for non-specialists (Larocco, 2024).

Summary and Reflections

In this chapter, we delved into the essential skills needed for conducting research in literature studies. We examined how to identify reliable sources, focusing on differentiating between scholarly articles and general sources. We also discussed the importance of formulating precise and insightful research questions to guide the research process effectively. Furthermore, we explored how integrating literary theory into research enriches analysis and offers deeper insights into texts.

We also covered practical strategies for organising research findings efficiently, such as categorising sources based on themes and utilising digital tools for citation management. This chapter emphasised the significance of maintaining academic integrity through proper attribution and avoiding plagiarism. By mastering these skills, students are well-equipped to conduct thorough research, compose well-structured essays, and confidently navigate the publishing process.

Reference List

Caulfield, J. (2020, January 30). *How to Write a Literary Analysis Essay | A Step-by-Step Guide.* Scribbr. https://www.scribbr.com/academic-essay/literary-analysis/

George, T. (2021, October 10). *How to Avoid Plagiarism with 3 Easy Steps*. Scribbr. https://www.scribbr.com/plagiarism/how-to-avoid-plagiarism/

How to write a journal article - Tips and Structure Guide. (n.d.). Author Services. https://authorservices.taylorandfrancis.com/publishing-your-research/writing-your-paper/writing-a-journal-article/

Larocco, C. (2024, July 9). *It's Not About the Research: How to Write for a General Audience When Academia Is All You Know | Jane Friedman*. Jane Friedman. https://janefriedman.com/its-not-about-the-research-how-to-write-for-a-general-audience-when-academia-is-all-you-know/

Literary Analysis Essay | EssayPro Blog. (2024). Essaypro.com. https://essaypro.com/blog/how-to-write-a-literary-analysis-essay

MIT Libraries. (2019). *LibGuides: Citing sources: Overview*. Mit.edu. https://libguides.mit.edu/citing

Research Guides: Organizing Your Social Sciences Research Paper: 11. Citing Sources. (2012). Usc.edu. https://libguides.usc.edu/writingguide/citingsources

Snyder, H. (2019, November). *Literature review as a research methodology: An overview and guidelines*. Journal of Business Research; ScienceDirect. https://www.sciencedirect.com/science/article/pii/S0148296319304564

ScoreDetect Blog | Data & Content Authenticity Technology. (2024, February 9). ScoreDetect Blog | Data & Content Authenticity Technology. https://www.scoredetect.com/blog/posts/preventing-plagiarism-in-academic-writing-best-practices

University of Southern California. (2019). *Research Guides: Organizing Your Social Sciences Research Paper: 5. The Literature Review*. Usc.edu. https://libguides.usc.edu/writingguide/literaturereview

To Readers

Throughout this book, we have embarked on an expansive journey through literature's multifaceted nature, exploring its foundational definitions and delving into the intricate worlds of diverse genres, periods, and movements. Each chapter has offered insights into literature's enduring impact on human experience, tracing its evolution from the rich landscapes of British literature to the innovative strides of modernity. Our exploration has unearthed the thematic richness of literary works and illuminated their profound role in reflecting and shaping society.

We began with the essential question: What is literature? Understanding literature as more than just written texts, we consider it a vast and dynamic mode of human expression. From ancient epics to contemporary novels, literature encompasses a spectrum of narratives that capture the complexities of human life. By examining various genres, including poetry, drama, and prose, we uncovered the unique characteristics that define them and their contributions to the literary tapestry.

Studying periods and movements revealed how literature evolves alongside historical and cultural shifts. We saw how the Renaissance revived classical ideals, Romanticism celebrated emotion and nature, and Modernism broke from tradition to experiment with new forms and perspectives. These movements underscore literature's adaptability and ability to resonate with readers across different eras.

A significant theme throughout our study has been the enduring impact of literature on human experience. Literature offers a mirror to society, reflecting its values, conflicts, and aspirations. It gives voice to marginalised communities, challenges prevailing norms, and fosters empathy by allowing us to see the world through others' eyes. Whether exploring themes of love, struggle, or identity, literature connects us to the broader human condition.

As we reflect on the importance of literature, it becomes clear that it is not merely an art form but a vital tool for understanding ourselves and the world around us. Literature invites us to think critically about our lives and societies, encouraging us to question, analyse, and appreciate diverse perspectives. Through literature, we access many experiences beyond our own, enriching our understanding of humanity's trials and triumphs.

Consider the power of a single story to shift perspectives. A novel in a distant culture can illuminate unfamiliar customs and beliefs, fostering cross-cultural understanding. A poem capturing a moment of intense emotion can resonate deeply, offering solace or inspiration. Literature enables us to travel through time and space, connecting with people and places we might never encounter otherwise.

Moreover, literature challenges us to confront complex issues and moral dilemmas. It compels us to grapple with justice, freedom, and identity questions, pushing us to consider our roles within larger societal frameworks. Literature enhances our critical thinking skills, teaching us to analyse, interpret, and engage thoughtfully with the world.

But this journey doesn't end here. This book serves as a starting point for your literary exploration. The world of literature is vast and ever-changing, offering endless opportunities for discovery. I encourage you to continue your engagement with texts, seeking out new authors, genres, and themes. Join local book clubs or online literary communities to share your insights and learn from others. Attend readings, workshops, and lectures to deepen your appreciation of the literary arts.

The skills and knowledge gained from this book will serve as a solid foundation for those pursuing further studies. Engage with academic journals, attend conferences, and seek mentorship from seasoned scholars. Explore interdisciplinary approaches, connecting literature with fields such as history, psychology, and sociology to enrich your analyses.

If you're inspired to write, use the pen (or keyboard) and contribute your voice to the literary conversation. Experiment with different forms and styles; be bold and tackle bold subjects. Your unique perspectives and experiences can add valuable insights to the literary landscape.

Remember the critical thinking and analytical skills we've discussed as you continue your journey. These tools are essential for engaging deeply with literary texts and appreciating their nuances. When reading, consider the author's context, the work's themes, and its broader implications. Ask questions, challenge assumptions, and seek more profound meanings. Great literature invites great questions—embrace this curiosity and let it guide your exploration.

In conclusion, literature is a powerful and transformative force, offering windows into the diverse fabric of human existence. It challenges us to think, feel, and connect in ways that enrich our lives and broaden our horizons. Whether you are an undergraduate student, an adult learner, or an educator, literature has something profound to offer. It is a journey without end, constantly evolving and expanding with each discovery.

Let this book be the beginning of your lifelong engagement with literature. Embrace the stories, voices, and perspectives that await you. Dive into the pages of a new novel, dissect a poem's intricacies, or revisit a timeless classic with fresh eyes. The world of literature is yours to explore, and I hope you find as much joy and enlightenment in it as countless readers and writers have before you.

Thank you for joining me on this journey through the realms of literature. May your future readings be filled with wonder, insight, and inspiration. Keep questioning, keep exploring, and above all, keep reading. The universe of literature awaits your unique interpretation and contribution.